Training for Certification

Taking an ASE Certification

This study guide will help prepare you to take and pass the ASE test. It contains descriptions of the types of questions used on the test, the task list from which the test questions are derived, a review of the task list subject information, and a practice test containing ASE style questions.

ABOUT ASE

The National Institute for Automotive Service Excellence (ASE) is a non-profit organization founded in 1972 for the purpose of improving the quality of automotive service and repair through the voluntary testing and certification of automotive technicians. Currently, there are over 400,000 professional technicians certified by ASE in over 40 different specialist areas.

ASE certification recognizes your knowledge and experience, and since it is voluntary, taking and passing an ASE certification test also demonstrates to employers and customers your commitment to your profession. It can mean better compensation and increased employment opportunities as well.

ASE not only certifies technician competency, it also promotes the benefits of technician certification to the motoring public. Repair shops that employ at least one ASE technician can display the ASE sign. Establishments where 75 percent of technicians are certified, with at least one technician certified in each area of service offered by the business, are eligible for the ASE Blue Seal of Excellence program. ASE encourages consumers to patronize these shops through media campaigns and car care clinics.

To become ASE certified, you must pass at least one ASE exam and have at least two years of related work experience. Technicians that pass specified tests in a series earn Master Technician status. Your certification is valid for five years, after which time you must retest to retain certification, demonstrating that you have kept up with the changing technology in the field.

THE ASE TEST

An ASE test consists of forty to eighty multiple-choice questions. Test questions are written by a panel of technical experts from vehicle, parts and equipment manufacturers, as well as working technicians and technical education instructors. All questions have been pre-tested and quality checked on a national sample of technicians. The questions are derived from information presented in the task list, which details the knowledge that a technician must have to pass an ASE test and be recognized as competent in that category. The task list is periodically updated by

---

© *Advanstar Communications Inc. 2012.3*
Customer Service 1-800-240-1968
FAX 218-740-6437
E-mail PassTheASE@advanstar.com
URL: www.PassTheASE.com
T5 - SUSPENSION & STEERING

Taking An ASE Certification Test

ASE in response to changes in vehicle technology and repair techniques.

There are five types of questions on an ASE test:
- Direct, or Completion
- MOST Likely
- Technician A and Technician B
- EXCEPT
- LEAST Likely

Direct, or Completion

This type of question is the kind that is most familiar to anyone who has taken a multiple-choice test: you must answer a direct question or complete a statement with the correct answer. There are four choices given as potential answers, but only one is correct. Sometimes the correct answer to one of these questions is clear, however in other cases more than one answer may seem to be correct. In that case, read the question carefully and choose the answer that is most correct. Here is an example of this type of test question:

A compression test shows that one cylinder is too low. A leakage test on that cylinder shows that there is excessive leakage. During the test, air could be heard coming from the tailpipe. Which of the following could be the cause?
A. broken piston rings
B. bad head gasket
C. bad exhaust gasket
D. an exhaust valve not seating

There is only one correct answer to this question, answer D. If an exhaust valve is not seated, air will leak from the combustion chamber by way of the valve out to the tailpipe and make an audible sound. Answer C is wrong because an exhaust gasket has nothing to do with combustion chamber sealing. Answers A and B are wrong because broken rings or a bad head gasket would have air leaking through the oil filler or coolant system.

MOST Likely

This type of question is similar to a direct question but it can be more challenging because all or some of the answers may be nearly correct. However, only one answer is the most correct. For example:

When a cylinder head with an overhead camshaft is discovered to be warped, which of the following is the most correct repair option?
A. replace the head
B. check for cracks, straighten the head, surface the head
C. surface the head, then straighten it
D. straighten the head, surface the head, check for cracks

The most correct answer is B. It makes no sense to perform repairs on a cylinder head that might not be usable. The head should first be checked for warpage and cracks. Therefore, answer B is more correct than answer D. The head could certainly be replaced, but the cost factor may be prohibitive and availability may be limited, so answer B is more correct than answer A. If the top of the head is warped enough to interfere with cam bore alignment and/or restrict free movement of the camshaft, the head must be straightened before it is resurfaced, so answer C is wrong.

Technician A and Technician B

These questions are the kind most commonly associated with the ASE test. With these questions you are asked to choose which technician statement is correct, or whether they both are correct or incorrect. This type of question can be difficult because very often you may find one technician's statement to be clearly correct or incorrect while the other may not be so obvious. Do you choose one technician or both? The key to answering these questions is to carefully examine each technician's statement independently and judge it on its own merit. Here is an example of this type of question:

A vehicle equipped with rack-and-pinion steering is having the front end inspected. Technician A says that the inner tie rod ends should be inspected while in their normal running position. Technician B says that if movement is felt between the tie rod stud and the socket while the tire is moved in and out, the inner tie rod should be replaced. Who is correct?
A. Technician A
B. Technician B
C. Both A and B
D. Neither A or B

The correct answer is C; both technicians' statements are correct. Technician B is clearly correct because any play felt between the tie-rod stud and the socket while the tire is moved in and out indicates that the assembly is worn and requires replacement. However, Technician A is also correct because inner tie-rods should be inspected while in their normal running position, to prevent binding that may occur when the suspension is allowed to hang free.

EXCEPT

This kind of question is sometimes called a negative question because you are asked to give the incorrect answer. All of the possible answers given are correct EXCEPT one. In effect, the correct answer to the question is the one that is wrong. The word EXCEPT is always capitalized in these questions. For example:

All of the following are true of torsion bars **EXCEPT**:
A. They can be mounted longitudi-

nally or transversely.
B. They serve the same function as coil springs.
C. They are interchangeable from side-to-side
D. They can be used to adjust vehicle ride height.

The correct answer is C. Torsion bars are not normally interchangeable from side-to-side. This is because the direction of the twisting or torsion is not the same on the left and right sides. All of the other answers contain true statements regarding torsion bars.

LEAST Likely

This type of question is similar to EXCEPT in that once again you are asked to give the answer that is wrong. For example:

Blue-gray smoke comes from the exhaust of a vehicle during deceleration. Of the following, which cause is **LEAST** likely?
A. worn valve guides
B. broken valve seals
C. worn piston rings
D. clogged oil return passages

The correct answer is C. Worn piston rings will usually make an engine smoke worse under acceleration. All of the other causes can allow oil to be drawn through the valve guides under the high intake vacuum that occurs during deceleration.

PREPARING FOR THE ASE TEST

Begin preparing for the test by reading the task list. The task list describes the actual work performed by a technician in a particular specialty area. Each question on an ASE test is derived from a task or set of tasks in the list. Familiarizing yourself with the task list will help you to concentrate on the areas where you need to study.

The text section of this study guide contains information pertaining to each of the tasks in the task list. Reviewing this information will prepare you to take the practice test.

Take the practice test and compare your answers with the correct answer explanations. If you get an answer wrong and don't understand why, go back and read the information pertaining to that question in the text.

After reviewing the tasks and the subject information and taking the practice test, you should be prepared to take the ASE test or be aware of areas where further study is needed. When studying with this study guide or any other source of information, use the following guidelines to make sure the time spent is as productive as possible:
- Concentrate on the subject areas where you are weakest.
- Arrange your schedule to allow specific times for studying.
- Study in an area where you will not be distracted.
- Don't try to study after a full meal or when you are tired.
- Don't wait until the last minute and try to 'cram' for the test.

REGISTERING FOR ASE COMPUTER-BASED TESTING

Registration for the ASE CBT tests can be done online in myASE or over the phone. While not mandatory, it is recommended that you establish a myASE account on the ASE website (www.ase.com). This can be a big help in managing the ASE certification process, as your test scores and certification expiry dates are all listed there.

Test times are available during two-month windows with a one-month break in between. This means that there is a total of eight months over the period of the calendar year that ASE testing is available.

Testing can be scheduled during the daytime, night, and weekends for maximum flexibility. Also, results are available immediately after test completion. Printed certificates are mailed at the end of the two-month test window. If you fail a test, you will not be allowed to register for the same test until the next two-month test window.

TAKING THE ASE TEST – COMPUTER-BASED TESTING (CBT)

On test day, bring some form of photo identification with you and be sure to arrive at the test center 30 minutes early to give sufficient time to check in. Once you have checked in, the test supervisor will issue you some scratch paper and pencils, as well as a composite vehicle test booklet if you are taking advanced tests. You will then be seated at a computer station and given a short online tutorial on how to complete the ASE CBT tests. You may skip the tutorial if you are already familiar with the CBT process.

The test question format is similar to those found in written ASE tests. Regular certification tests have a time limit of 1 to 2 hours, depending on the test. Recertification tests are 30 to 45 minutes, and the L1 and L2 advanced level tests are capped at 2 hours. The time remaining for your test is displayed on the top left of the test window. You are given a warning when you have 5 minutes left to complete the test.

Read through each question carefully. If you don't know the answer to a question and need to think about it, click on the "Flag" button and move on to the next question. You may also go back to previous questions by pressing the "Previous Question" button. Don't spend too much time on any one

Taking An ASE Certification Test

question. After you have worked through to the end of the test, check your remaining time and go back and answer the questions you flagged. Very often, information found in questions later in the test can help answer some of the ones with which you had difficulty.

Some questions may have more content than what can fit on one screen. If this is the case, there will be a "More" button displayed where the "Next Question" button would ordinarily appear. A scrolling bar will also appear, showing what part of the question you are currently viewing. Once you have viewed all of the related content for the question, the "Next Question" button will reappear.

You can change answers on any of the questions before submitting the test for scoring. At the end of the examination, you will be shown a table with all of the question numbers. This table will show which questions are answered, which are unanswered, and which have been flagged for review. You will be given the option to review all the questions, review the flagged questions, or review the unanswered questions from this page. This table can be reviewed at any time during the exam by clicking the "Review" button.

If you are running out of time and still have unanswered test questions, guess the answers if necessary to make sure every question is answered. Do not leave any answers blank. It is to your advantage to answer every question, because your test score is based on the number of correct answers. A guessed answer could be correct, but a blank answer can never be.

Once you are satisfied that all of the questions are complete and ready for scoring, click the "Submit for Scoring" button. If you are scheduled for more than one test, the next test will begin immediately. If you are done with testing, you will be asked to complete a short survey regarding the CBT test experience. As you are leaving the test center, your supervisor will give you a copy of your test results. Your scores will also be available on myASE within two business days.

To learn exactly where and when the ASE Certification Tests are available in your area, as well as the costs involved in becoming ASE certified, please contact ASE directly for registration information.

The National Institute for Automotive Service Excellence
101 Blue Seal Drive, S.E. Suite 101
Leesburg, VA 20175
1-800-390-6789
http://www.ase.com

Table of Contents
T5 - Suspension & Steering

Test Specifications And Task List 6

Steering System Diagnosis And Repair 9

Suspension System Diagnosis And Repair 26

Wheel Alignment Diagnosis, Adjustment And Repair 43

Wheels And Tires Diagnosis And Repair 52

Sample Test Questions 61

Answers to Study-Guide Test Questions 70

Glossary 78

Advanstar endeavors to collect and include complete, correct and current information in this publication but does not warrant that any or all of such information is complete, correct or current. Publisher does not assume, and hereby disclaims, any liability to any person or entity for any loss or damage caused by errors or omissions of any kind, whether resulting from negligence, accident or any other cause. If you do notice any error, we would appreciate if you would bring such error to our attention.

Test Specifications And Task List

Medium/Heavy Truck Suspension And Steering

TEST SPECIFICATIONS FOR MEDIUM/HEAVY SUSPENSION AND STEERING (TEST T5)

CONTENT AREA	NUMBER OF QUESTIONS IN ASE TEST	PERCENTAGE OF COVERAGE IN ASE TEST
A. Steering System Diagnosis And Repair	12	24%
B. Suspension, Frame and 5th wheel Diagnosis And Repair	16	32%
C. Wheel Alignment Diagnosis, Adjustment And Repair	13	26%
D. Wheels And Tires Diagnosis And Repair	9	18%
TOTAL	**50**	**100%**

The 5-year Recertification Test will cover the same content areas as those listed above. However, the number of questions in each content area of the Recertification Test will be reduced by about one-half.

The following pages list the tasks covered in each content area. These task descriptions offer detailed information to technicians preparing for the test and persons who may be instructing Medium/Heavy-Duty Steering and Suspension technicians. This task list may also serve as a guideline for question writers, reviewers and test assemblers.

It should be noted that the number of questions in each content area might not equal the number of tasks listed. Some of the tasks are complex and broad in scope, and may be covered by several questions. Other tasks are simple and narrow in scope; one question may cover several tasks. The main purpose for listing the tasks is to describe accurately what is done on the job, not to make each task correspond to a particular test question.

MEDIUM/HEAVY DUTY TRUCK SUSPENSION AND STEERING TEST TASK LIST

A. STEERING SYSTEM DIAGNOSIS AND REPAIR
(12 questions)

Task 1 - Diagnose steering column (tilt telescoping, or fixed) for noise, looseness, and binding problems; determine needed repairs.

Task 2 - Inspect and replace steering shaft U-joint(s), slip joints, bearings, bushings and seals; phase shaft U-joints.

Task 3 - Check cab mounting and adjust ride height.

Task 4 - Remove the steering wheel (includes steering wheels equipped with electrical/electronic controls and components); install and center the steering wheel. Inspect, test, replace, and calibrate steering angle sensors.

Task 5 - Diagnose power steering system noise, steering binding, darting/oversteer, reduced wheel cut, steering wheel kick, pulling, non-recovery, turning effort, looseness, hard steering, overheating, fluid leakage and fluid aeration problems; determine needed repairs.

Task 6 - Determine recommended type of power steering fluid; check level and condition; determine needed service.

Task 7 - Flush and refill power steering system; purge air from system.

Task 8 - Perform power steering system pressure, temperature and flow tests; determine needed repairs.

Task 9 - Inspect, service or replace power steering fluid reservoir including filter, seals and gaskets.

Task 10 - Inspect, and reinstall/replace power steering pump drive belts, pulleys and tensioners; adjust drive belts and check alignment.

Task 11 - Inspect, adjust, or replace power steering pump, drive gears/shafts, mountings, and brackets.

Task 12 - Inspect and replace power steering system cooler, lines, hoses, clamps/mountings, fittings; check hose routing.

Task 13 - Inspect, adjust or replace linkage-assist type power steering cylinder or gear (dual system).

Task 14 - Inspect, adjust, repair or replace integral type power steer-

ing gear.
Task 15 - Adjust manual and automatic steering gear poppet/relief valves.
Task 16 - Inspect, align, and replace pitman arm.
Task 17 - Inspect, adjust or replace drag link (relay rod) and tie-rod ends (ball and adjustable socket type).
Task 18 - Inspect and replace steering arm.
Task 19 - Inspect and replace tie rod cross tube (relay rod/center link), clamps, and retainers; position as needed.

B. SUSPENSION SYSTEM DIAGNOSIS AND REPAIR
(16 questions)

Task 1 - Inspect and replace front axle beam and mounting hardware.
Task 2 - Inspect, service, adjust or replace kingpin, bushings, locks, bearings, seals and covers.
Task 3 - Inspect and replace shock absorbers, bushings, brackets and mounts.
Task 4 - Inspect, repair, and replace (leaf and parabolic) springs, center bolts, clips, spring eye bolts and bushings, shackles, slippers, insulators, brackets, and mounts.
Task 5 - Inspect, adjust or replace axle aligning devices including radius rods/arms, transverse torque rods, transverse torque rods/track bars, stabilizer bars, bushings, mounts, shims and cams.
Task 6 - Inspect or replace walking beams, center (cross) tube, bushings, mounts, load pads, brackets, caps and mounting hardware.
Task 7 - Inspect, test, and replace air suspension springs (bags), mounting plates, and main support beams/springs, pressure regulator and height control valves, linkages, lines, hoses, and fittings.
Task 8 - Diagnose, inspect, and replace auxiliary lift axle components and controls.
Task 9 - Measure front and rear vehicle ride height; determine needed adjustments or repairs.
Task 10 - [not present]
Task 11 - Torque U-bolts to manufacturers' specification.
Task 12 - Check axle load distribution problems on rear suspensions; check axle seat planning angles and pinion angles.
Task 13 - Inspect frame and frame members for cracks, breaks, distortion, elongated holes, looseness, and damage; determine needed repairs.
Task 14 - Inspect, install, or repair frame hangers, brackets, crossmembers and fasteners in accordance with manufacturers' recommended procedures.
Task 15 - Inspect, adjust, service, repair, or replace fifth wheel, pivot pins, busings, locking jaw mechanisms, and mounting bolts.
Task 16 - Inspect, adjust, service, repair, or replace sliding fifth wheel, tracks, stops, locking systems, air cylinders, springs, lines, hoses, and controls.
Task 17 - Inspect, install, repair or replace pintle hooks and draw bars.

C. WHEEL ALIGNMENT DIAGNOSIS, ADJUSTMENT AND REPAIR
(13 questions)

Task 1 - Diagnose vehicle wandering, darting, pulling, drifting, shimmy, and steering effort problems; determine needed adjustments and repairs.
Task 2 - Check camber and KPI (kingpin inclination); determine needed repairs.
Task 3 - Check and adjust caster.
Task 4 - Check and adjust toe.
Task 5 - Check rear axle(s) alignment (thrustline/centerline) and tracking (lateral offset, parallelism); adjust or determine needed repairs.
Task 6 - Check turning/Ackerman angle (toe out on turns); and maximum turning radius (wheel cut); determine needed repairs.

D. WHEELS, TIRES AND HUB DIAGNOSIS AND REPAIR
(9 questions)

Task 1 - Diagnose tire wear patterns; determine needed repairs.
Task 2 - Diagnose wheel end vibration, shimmy, pounding, hop (tramp) problems; determine needed repairs.
Task 3 - Inspect and replace wheels, mounting hardware, studs, and fasteners.
Task 4 - Measure wheel and tire radial and lateral runout; determine needed repairs or adjustments.
Task 5 - Inspect tires; check and adjust air pressure to tire manufacturers' specifications.
Task 6 - Perform static balance of wheel and tire assembly.
Task 7 - Perform dynamic balance of wheel and tire assembly.
Task 8 - Measure tire diameter and match tires on tandem axle(s).
Task 9 - Remove and reinstall tire/wheel wheel assembly.
Task 10 - Clean, inspect, lubricate and replace wheel hubs; wheel bearings and races/cups; replace seals and wear rings; adjust wheel bearings (including one and two nut types) to manufacturers' specifications.
Task 11 - Task 11 – Inspect and replace unitized hub bearing assemblies; perform initial installation and maintenance procedures to manufacturers' specifications.

The preceding Task List Data details all of the related informational subject matter you are expected to know in order to sit for this ASE Certification Test. Your own years of experience in the professional automotive service repair trade as a technician also should provide you with added background.

Finally, a conscientious review of the self-study material provided in this Training for ASE Certification.

Notes

Steering System Diagnosis And Repair

The steering system in a medium or heavy-duty truck is subject to extreme loads due to the size of the vehicle and the amount of weight it carries. The steering system, in conjunction with the suspension system, must be properly maintained in order to allow for proper handling while driving.

STEERING COLUMN

WARNING: Before servicing the steering column, make sure the Supplemental Restraint System (SRS) air bag module circuit is fully deactivated. Follow the vehicle manufacturer's recommended procedure to deactivate and remove the air bag module. Always wear safety glasses.

Any time that a steering column or shaft is replaced, it is important to carefully inspect the old and new columns to be sure the designs are identical.

Steering columns are made to be collapsible to prevent the column from seriously impacting the driver during a front-end collision. If an accident has occurred, and the steering column has partially collapsed, the entire column must be replaced.

Most steering columns include U-joints or flexible couplings. Flexible couplings are typically called rag joints. Normally, a worn or damaged joint can be easily replaced. Most flex couplings are replaceable or rebuildable, and kits are available, but some flexible couplings are fixed parts of the column shaft and can't be replaced separately.

Trucks use an intermediate shaft that runs from the lower end of the column shaft to the steering gear input shaft, where it connects with a flex coupling or U-joint. In some cases, the upper end of the intermediate shaft is equipped with a U-joint, which is usually not replaceable or rebuildable.

Diagnosis

Steering column component malfunctions can cause binding, hard steering, looseness and excessive steering wheel play. Establish the complaint by getting as much information as possible from the driver. Remember, the driver is the first link (and sometimes the best) in the diagnostic chain. Next, give the vehicle a thorough road test.

When experiencing excessive wander, look for:
- Steering column shaft adjustment
- Worn upper or lower bearings
- Worn U-joint or flex coupling.

When experiencing no steering recovery, look for:
- Lack of lubrication in the U-joint or flex coupling
- Worn upper or lower bearings
- Bent steering shaft
- U-joints not installed properly or improperly phased.

When experiencing excessive steering wheel movement, look for:
- Loose steering wheel
- U-joint or flex coupling worn
- Loose steering gear
- Loose pitman arm
- Loose or worn steering linkage components
- Steering gear out of adjustment.

When experiencing steering column binding, look for:
- U-joint or flex coupling worn or seized
- Column bearings binding or misaligned
- Bent steering shaft
- U-joints not installed properly or improperly phased.

Removal

Disconnect the negative battery cable. Make sure the Supplemental Restraint System (SRS) air bag module circuit is fully deactivated. Follow the vehicle manufacturer's recommended procedure to deactivate and remove the air bag module. Remove any steering column and/or dash trim that will interfere with removal of the column assembly. Remove the steering wheel by removing the hub cover and unscrewing the steering wheel attachment nut. Using a suitable wheel puller, remove the steering wheel from the upper steering column

Training for Certification

Steering System Diagnosis And Repair

shaft. Reinstall the steering wheel nut to prevent the steering column shaft from sliding out of the jacket tube (if applicable). Remove any combination switches from the column.

CAUTION: Do not use a knock-off type steering wheel puller or strike the end of the upper shaft with a hammer. This will cause damage to the steering shaft bearing.

Remove the pinch bolt from the yoke at the end of the lower steering column shaft and separate the shaft from the yoke. Mark the position of the yoke and shaft for assembly reference.

Remove the turn signal control and trailer brake control (if equipped) from the column. Remove the lower bracket cover over the steering column U-joint or flex coupling. Remove any securing bolts or nuts that hold the column in place at the firewall. Unbolt the upper bracket holding the steering column in place under the dash, and lift the column from the vehicle.

Installation

Position the column in the vehicle and loosely install the dash bracket bolts or nuts. This will enable the column to be held in place while all other connections are made. Install any securing bolts or nuts that hold the column in place at the firewall. Install the lower bracket cover over the steering column U-joint or flex coupling. Reconnect the horn wire and install the turn signal control and trailer brake control (if equipped).

Install the yoke at the end of the steering column, aligning the marks made during removal. Install the pinch bolt. Install the steering wheel and use the vehicle manufacturer's recommended procedure for installing the air bag module. Torque all fasteners to manufacturer's specifications. Reconnect the negative battery cable.

Upper Bearing Replacement

Disconnect the negative battery cable. Make sure the Supplemental Restraint System (SRS) air bag module circuit is fully deactivated. Follow the vehicle manufacturer's recommended procedure to deactivate and remove the air bag module. Remove the necessary steering column and/or dash trim that will interfere with removal of the column assembly.

Unscrew the steering wheel attachment nut. Using a suitable wheel puller, remove the steering wheel from the upper steering column shaft

Loosen the pinch bolt and separate the yoke from the end of the shaft. Remove any tilt-column components (if equipped) that would impede removal of the upper bearing. Remove any combination switches from the column if necessary.

Remove the upper bearing retaining plate. Remove the fastener holding the upper bearing onto the steering shaft. Pull outward on the steering column shaft. It should move slightly, bringing the bearing and sleeve with it. Using a suitable prying tool, gently pry the bearing off the steering column shaft, using the steering column housing as a fulcrum.

Install the upper bearing onto the steering column shaft, positioning the bearing and insulator as far down on the upper shaft as possible. Place a suitable installation tool over the steering column upper shaft and install the steering wheel attaching nut.

Tighten the attaching nut until the bearing is seated completely on the shaft. Remove the steering wheel attaching nut and installation tool from the upper column shaft, and install the bearing fastener and its retaining plate. Reinstall tilt-column components and combination switches (if equipped) and connect the yoke to the shaft, making sure it is properly phased. Install the steering column and/or dash trim, and the steering wheel. Torque all fasteners to manufacturer's specifications.

Lower Shaft Replacement

Remove any protective shields from the shaft. Remove the fasteners attaching the lower steering column shaft to the lower shaft assembly, and slide the lower shaft out of the steering column shaft. Remove the pinch bolt from the yoke at the end of the shaft and separate the shaft from the yoke. Slide the lower shaft off the steering gear. At this time, any U-joints or flex couplings can be replaced.

Installation is the reverse of removal. Make sure the U-joint(s) on the lower shaft are properly phased (sometimes called 'clocked' or 'positioned') in relation to the steering shaft yoke to allow for sufficient operating angles. Phasing is the relative position of one yoke to another within a 360-degree revolution. Most U-joint yokes and slip joints are match marked as to be installed 180-degrees from each other. This eliminates Torsional Excitation, or winding up and unwinding of the shaft. Thus, phasing affects joint cancellation in that an incorrectly phased shaft will cause the shaft to bind, producing premature wear of components.

CAB MOUNTING

The cab mounting system connects the cab assembly to the vehicle frame and is designed to absorb shock, vibration, and lateral movement transmitted from the vehicle chassis. In addition, if equipped with air ride, the cab mounting system helps to ensure that the cab

Steering System Diagnosis And Repair

stays level.

A conventional system uses rubber or polyurethane bushings to isolate the cab from the frame. This type of setup offers sufficient dampening at a reasonable cost. The disadvantages to rubber or polyurethane bushings is that they are susceptible to outside elements and cannot compensate for cab ride height.

Inspect the bushings in accordance with the vehicle's preventive maintenance schedule. Look for evidence of cab shifting by taking measurements at the manufacturer's prescribed positions. Replace the cab mount bushing(s) if any abnormal wear or cab shifting is detected.

Check the cab air suspension (if equipped). A cab air suspension replaces the rear solid mounts on a truck cab, and is designed to absorb road vibrations, back slap, and harsh road jolts. Inspect the air bags (springs) for damage and wear, and make sure the cab shock absorbers are not leaking. Air lines should be routed properly with no kinks or damage. Inspect the valves and lines for leakage at the fittings. Valve mounting locations, and cab measurements will vary by manufacturer.

To check the cab height control valve operation, unhook the trailer and park the truck on a level surface. Run the engine and build up the air pressure to manufacturer's specification. Turn off the engine and apply the parking brake.

Disconnect the linkage from the height control valve and push down on the valve lever. If air passes through the intake of the valve, it is working correctly. The cab will rise and the flow of air will be audible. Now, pull the lever upwards. If air exhausts through the valve, the exhaust portion of the valve is working correctly. The cab will lower and the flow of air will be audible. If the valve checks out

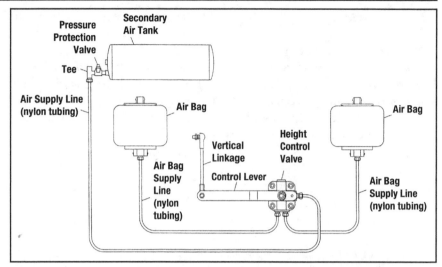

Cab air suspension components. *(Courtesy: Daimler Trucks North America)*

OK, reconnect the linkage.

Conditions that indicate required service include:
- Air leaks from the height control valve after the lever has returned to the neutral position.
- High air consumption indicating air exhausting excessively.
- An increase in the compressor duty cycle.
- Cab sitting too high or too low.

Cab Ride Height

Use the manufacturer's recommended procedures and measurement points to check cab ride height. As a general rule, measurements should be taken from the bottom of the cab to the frame assembly on all four corners. If you find any differences from side-to-side, front to back, or if the cab is higher or lower than specifications, adjust the cab ride height.

Cab ride height can be adjusted by starting the engine and allowing air pressure to build to manufacturer's specifications. Loosen the height control valve linkage and exhaust the air from the air bags. Move the height control valve lever to fill the air bags to the desired specification, and then tighten the height control linkage lock nut. Next, recheck cab ride height.

STEERING SYSTEM DIAGNOSIS

Steering system malfunctions can range from leaks, to specific component failures, or both. A good starting point when troubleshooting a power steering system is checking the performance of the system in terms of operating smoothness. Establish the complaint by getting as much information as possible from the driver. Remember, the driver is the first link (and sometimes the best) in the diagnostic chain.

When diagnosing a leak, clean the suspected area with an appropriate cleaning solution. Make sure the system has the right amount of power steering fluid in the reservoir. Always use the type of power steering fluid specified by the vehicle manufacturer. Start the vehicle and rotate the steering wheel from stop to stop, being careful not to hold the wheel against either stop for more than 2 seconds. Note the leak and repair as necessary.

Replenish the fluid and rotate the steering wheel from stop-to-stop, being careful not to hold the wheel against either stop for more than 2 seconds. If the symptoms still persist, air may need to be purged from the system, or the

Training for Certification

Steering System Diagnosis And Repair

pump may need replacing.

Warning: When the engine is running, the power steering fluid is under extreme pressure, which significantly raises its temperature. Injury can occur if adequate precautions are not followed.

When experiencing intermittent or no power steering assist, look for:
- Belt slipping and/or low fluid level
- Piston or rod binding in power cylinder (linkage-type)
- Sliding sleeve stuck in control valve (linkage-type)
- Pump flow control valve sticking.

When experiencing hard steering, look for:
- Low or uneven tire pressure
- Insufficient lubricant in steering gear housing or in steering linkage
- Steering gear adjustments too tight
- Improper alignment
- Steering column misaligned
- Loose, worn or broken pump belt
- Air in system
- Low fluid level in pump reservoir
- Pump output pressure flow
- Leakage at power cylinder piston rings
- Binding or bent cylinder linkage
- Valve spool and/or sleeve sticking
- Column shaft slip joint binding
- Sector shaft adjustment incorrect.

When experiencing excessive steering looseness, look for:
- Steering gear sector shaft adjusted too loose or shaft and/or bushing badly worn
- Excessive steering gear worm end-play due to bearing adjustment
- Steering linkage loose or worn
- Front wheel bearings improperly adjusted
- Steering arm loose on steering gear shaft
- Steering gear housing attaching bolts loose
- Steering arms loose
- Worn kingpins or bushings
- Loose spring shackles
- Drag link or tie-rod ends worn
- Sector shaft adjustment incorrect due to adjusting with steering linkage connected.

When the vehicle darts out of a steered line or oversteers, look for:
- Poorly lubricated steering gear, axle or steering system
- Steering gear mountings loose at frame
- Pitman arm loose on steering box output shaft
- Steering gearbox distorted due to uneven frame mounting surface
- Drag link ends binding or loose
- Drag link of improper length (makes box operate off-center)
- Improper toe-in
- Axle U-bolts loose (allowing axle to shift on springs)
- Weak or broken springs, damaged air bags, worn shackle pins/bushings anywhere in suspension system
- Loose lug nuts
- Loose tie-rod ball joints, tie-rod arms or steering arm
- Broken/loose engine mounts
- Vehicle load very poorly distributed
- Tandem front axle misaligned
- Worn wheel bearings
- Excessive front wheel brake drag
- Twisted, sprung or diamond-shaped frame
- Kingpin or kingpin thrust bearing loose, binding or seized
- Bent axle.

When the steering exhibits poor or no recovery from turns, look for:
- Improper caster or toe settings
- Steering gear adjustments too tight
- Improper spool nut adjustment (linkage-type)
- Valve spool installed backwards (linkage-type)
- Low tire pressure
- Tight steering linkage
- Kingpins seized.

When experiencing high steering effort in one direction, look for:
- Unequal tire pressures
- Vehicle overloaded
- Hydraulic system pressure too low
- High internal leakage in the steering box in one direction only.

When experiencing high steering effort in both directions, look for:
- Tire pressure low
- Wheel spindle bent
- Manual steering assembly binding or misadjusted
- Power steering unit has low pump pressure due to a defective relief valve, low fluid level, slipping belt or hydraulic control problem. Steering slave unit may have worn internal parts
- Tie-rod ends tight
- Caster excessive
- Kingpins or ball joints too tight
- Lack of lubrication to steering and suspension units
- Tractor-trailer fifth wheel damaged or galled, improperly lubricated or improperly positioned
- Axle U-bolts loose so axle shifts and becomes improperly

Steering System Diagnosis And Repair

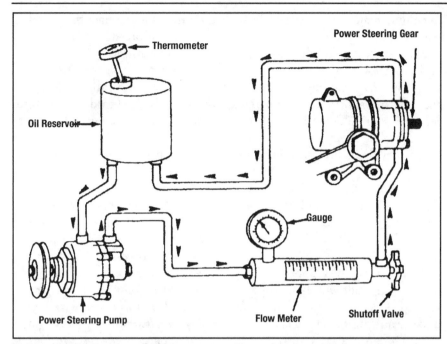

Testing a Bendix power steering system for pressure and flow. *(Courtesy: Bendix Corp.)*

aligned
- Loose wheel lugnuts
- Very loose tie-rod ball joints, tie-rod arms, steering arms (so alignment becomes poor)
- Misadjusted (dragging) front brakes.

When experiencing excessive play in the steering wheel, look for:
- Wheel loose on steering shaft
- Loose connection (U-joint) among steering gear, intermediate column and steering column
- Steering gear improperly bolted to frame
- Pitman arm loose on output shaft
- Worn steering linkage components

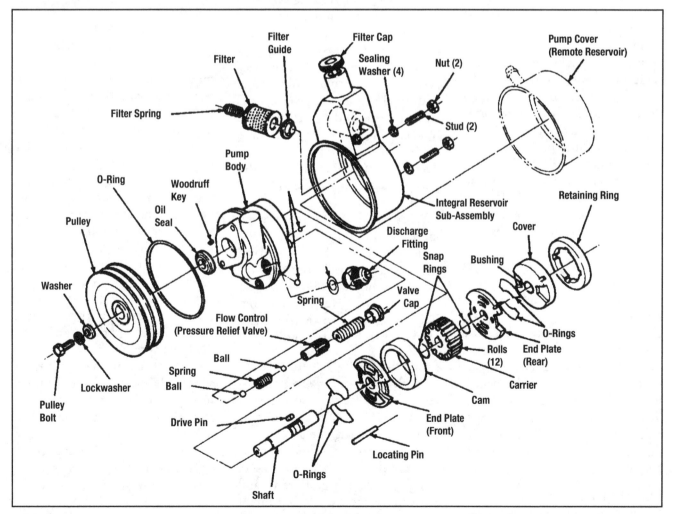

Exploded view of Eaton power steering pump with integral reservoir. *(Courtesy: Eaton Corp.)*

Training for Certification 13

Steering System Diagnosis And Repair

- Steering gear improperly adjusted.

If the steering system runs too hot, look for:
- Pump flow too high
- Vehicle overloaded
- Replacement hose too small in diameter, or correct hose is kinked, bent to severe angle or clogged
- Steering column binds or input shaft has side load due to misalignment (keeps gear valve from recentering properly when truck runs straight ahead)
- Poppet malfunctioning
- Prolonged stationary vehicle operation.

Power Steering Fluid

Always use the type of power steering fluid specified by the vehicle manufacturer, since fluid requirements may vary from one vehicle to another. Once a specific fluid type is established, it should never be mixed with any other type. If it is necessary to change the type of fluid, or the fluid becomes contaminated or discolored due to a failure, the entire system must be drained and flushed.

When checking the power steering fluid, make sure the vehicle is parked on a level surface. Inspect the power steering filler cap area and wipe away dirt with a clean shop rag. Run the engine until it reaches operating temperature. Shut the engine down and remove the dipstick from the reservoir. Wipe the dipstick clean and reinstall it into the reservoir. Wait a few seconds and then remove the dipstick to read the fluid level. Specific notches or indicators on the dipstick will indicate the appropriate levels.

Flushing The System

When checking the power steering fluid, make sure the vehicle is parked on a level surface. Inspect the power steering filler cap area and wipe away dirt with a clean shop rag. Run the engine until it reaches operating temperature. Shut the engine down and remove the dipstick from the reservoir. Wipe the dipstick clean and reinstall it into the reservoir. Wait a few seconds and then remove the dipstick to read the fluid level. Specific notches or indicators on the dipstick will indicate the appropriate levels.

Raise and safely support the vehicle so the front wheels are off the ground. Place a suitable drain pan underneath the vehicle to catch the fluid. Disconnect the return line at the outlet port of the steering gear.

Fill the power steering reservoir and disable the ignition system so the vehicle does not start. Always use the type of power steering fluid specified by the vehicle manufacturer. Turn the engine over while adding fluid as the level drops. Continue to add fluid until the fluid coming out of the return hose is clear of contamination. Reconnect the return line at the outlet port of the steering gear and fill the system.

When the fluid level is at the full mark on the dipstick, enable the ignition and start the engine. Turn the steering wheel from stop-to-stop until the air bubbles disappear from the power steering reservoir. Fill the reservoir to the full mark on the dipstick or reservoir.

Pressure/Temperature Test

Be sure the fluid level is correct and the fluid temperature is at least 176°F (80°C). A suitable thermometer may be inserted in the pump reservoir fluid to measure the fluid temperature. Install a high-pressure shutoff valve and pressure gauge on the output of the pump. Be careful not to leave the valve closed longer than it takes to read the pressure gauge, as the fluid will overheat.

To perform the pressure test, have the engine idling, close the shutoff valve and read the pressure. It should meet the pump manufacturer's minimum specification, or the pump or relief valve must be repaired.

WARNING: Do not allow the fluid to become too hot during the power steering pump pressure test. Excessively high fluid temperature reduces pump pressure. Wear protective gloves and always shut the engine off before disconnecting gauge fittings, because the hot fluid may cause burns.

Flow Test

Be sure the fluid level is correct and the fluid temperature is at least 176°F (80°C). A suitable thermometer may be inserted in the pump reservoir fluid to measure the fluid temperature. After the first portion of the test, allow fluid to return to 125° (52° C) to 135°F (57° C).

Install a suitable flow measuring valve on the output of the pump. To begin the test, have the engine idling and read the flow rate with the load valve open. Compare the reading with the manufacturer's specification. Then close the load valve. Now, the flow meter should move to zero and the pressure gauge should read the pump's specified relief pressure.

Quickly open the load valve again. The reading should immediately return to the value read before with the load valve open. If it doesn't, this indicates a problem with the pump that could cause an intermittent loss of power assist.

Repeat the above test with the engine at governed rpm.

Steering System Diagnosis And Repair

Power Steering Reservoir

All power steering systems are supplied with fluid from a reservoir that is either built onto the pump or remotely mounted. The reservoir is the fluid sump for the power steering system. It contains enough fluid to supply the normal operating needs of the system, plus an additional supply to replace fluid lost through minor leakage. Although the function of the reservoir is to supply an adequate amount of fluid to the system, it is more than just a vessel containing fluid. It is in the reservoir that the fluid has the greatest potential danger of becoming contaminated.

Remote Mounted Reservoir

The remote reservoir tank is mounted inside the engine compartment. Power steering pump suction and return lines are attached to the reservoir. The remote reservoir should be located in a position that allows downward flow of fluid to the power steering pump. This creates a constant flow of fluid and decreases the chance of fluid cavitation.

Most reservoirs are vented to the atmosphere through an opening that allows air to exit or enter the space above the oil as the oil level rises or falls. A filler/breather unit containing a filtering element is often incorporated with the vent. It must be large enough to handle the air flow required to maintain atmospheric pressure whether the tank is full or empty.

Replacement of a leaky reservoir consists of simply placing a suitable drain pan underneath the reservoir, disconnecting the lines and allowing the remaining fluid to drain, then removing the reservoir assembly from its mounting bracket.

Pump Mounted Reservoir

The pump-mounted power steering reservoir performs the same function as the remote reservoir, supplying power steering fluid to the pump assembly. On most vehicles, the reservoir assembly is attached to the pump with retaining nuts. The reservoir is sealed to the pump using a reservoir gasket or O-ring. Leakage usually occurs at the gasket or O-ring, or from some type of external damage to the reservoir housing.

Replacement of the pump mounted reservoir entails removing the pump assembly from the vehicle, and removing the retaining nuts that secure the reservoir to the pump.

Separate the reservoir from the pump housing. If the reservoir is sealed by a gasket, clean the sealing surfaces and replace the gasket with a new one. If it is sealed by an O-ring, remove and discard the old seal. Lubricate a new seal with an appropriate lubricant and carefully install it in the pump housing. Reinstall the reservoir, making sure the gasket or O-ring seals the entire circumference of the housing. Reinstall the pump assembly.

POWER STEERING BELTS

Squealing noises from the engine compartment that increase in frequency as the engine rpm is raised, or when the steering wheel is turned, can usually be attributed to loose or worn belt(s). Loose belt tension can cause lack of power assist in a steering system.

Causes of belt failure include:
- Insufficient tension—Belt slippage produces heat, allowing the belt to stiffen, lessening its gripping power
- No run-in and retension—Newly installed belts should be run with the engine at high idle for a few minutes. Afterwards, the belt should be retensioned

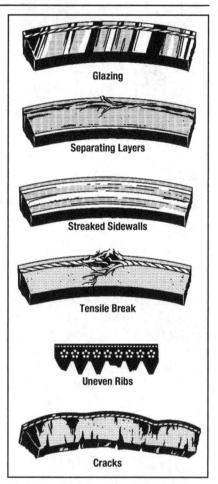

Conditions that require drive belt replacement.
(Courtesy: Daimler Trucks North America)

- No periodic maintenance—Gradual loss of belt tension occurs over time. That's why belt inspection should be part of any preventive maintenance program
- Change in bracket or pulley geometry—As brackets and pulleys flex or bend, distances will change, resulting in tension loss.

Belt tension checks should be performed using a belt tension gauge. Check the belt at a point midway between pulleys on the longest belt span. In multi-belt drives, the belt tension readings taken on the same span may vary considerably between belts. When this occurs, average out the readings to achieve the applied tension.

Steering System Diagnosis And Repair

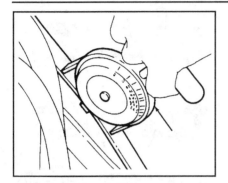

Using a handheld gauge to check belt tension.
(Courtesy: Ford Motor Co.)

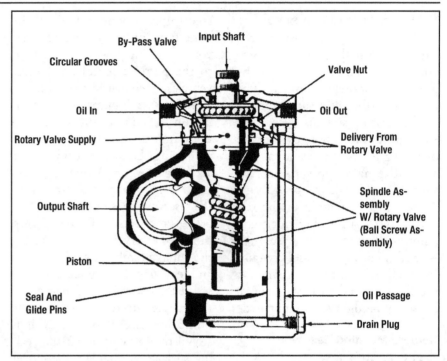

Cross section of Bendix integral steering gear.   *(Courtesy: Bendix Corp.)*

Removal And Installation

When identical belts are used on the same drive, they must be replaced as matched sets. When replacing belt(s), loosen the belt tensioner or pivot, and remove the belt. Never pry the belt from a pulley. After the belt is removed, spin the pulley to determine if it wobbles or has imperfections such as bearing wear.

NOTE: Depending on the particular configuration, additional belts may have to be removed to gain access to the power steering belt(s).

Install the new belt by correctly positioning it in its pulley grooves. In the case of automatically tensioned belts, move the tensioner to a position where the belt can be installed onto the pulleys. In the case of pivot style tensioning, use the proper tools to move the appropriate tensioner pivot. The belt(s) should not bottom in the pulley grooves or excessively protrude from the pulley radius.

Start the engine and make sure the belt(s) are not running against any adjacent parts of the engine. Check pulley alignment using manufacturer's recommendations and specifications. If pulleys are misaligned, look for improper positioning of the power steering pump or its corresponding pulley(s), improper fit of the pulley or shaft, or incorrect components installed.

POWER STEERING PUMP

The power steering pump controls the hydraulic fluid flow throughout the power steering system. The pump can be either gear or belt driven, depending on the manufacturer, and can come in two internal configurations, roller or vane.

The pump should be tested if there is a lack of hydraulic pressure. Low pressure can be caused either by pump problems or by problems in the steering gear. Pump tests tell the technician which part is causing the problem. A complete test of the pump requires checking both pressure and volume. Flow and pressure meters are installed on the complete system. After testing for both flow capacity and pressure, evaluate the results.

When the power steering pump lacks the ability to perform its primary function properly, is low on fluid or when air is introduced into the system, a whining noise will usually be heard coming from the pump. This can be accompanied by increased turning effort, binding, non-recovery, pump overheating and hard steering.

If pressure is low and the flow is low, suspect a faulty power steering pump. If pressure is low but the flow is normal, chances are that excessive internal clearance in the steering gear, due to wear, is causing the problem.

Clean excessive dirt, oil and debris from around the pump. Power steering pump mounting bolts must be checked for proper torque, and brackets must not be missing or damaged. If the pump is belt driven, the belt must be inspected and tightened to manufacturer's specifications.

Check to see if there is an adequate amount of the proper fluid in the reservoir. Always use the type of power steering fluid specified by the vehicle manufacturer. Check the condition of the fluid, noting any discoloration. Air in the

Steering System Diagnosis And Repair

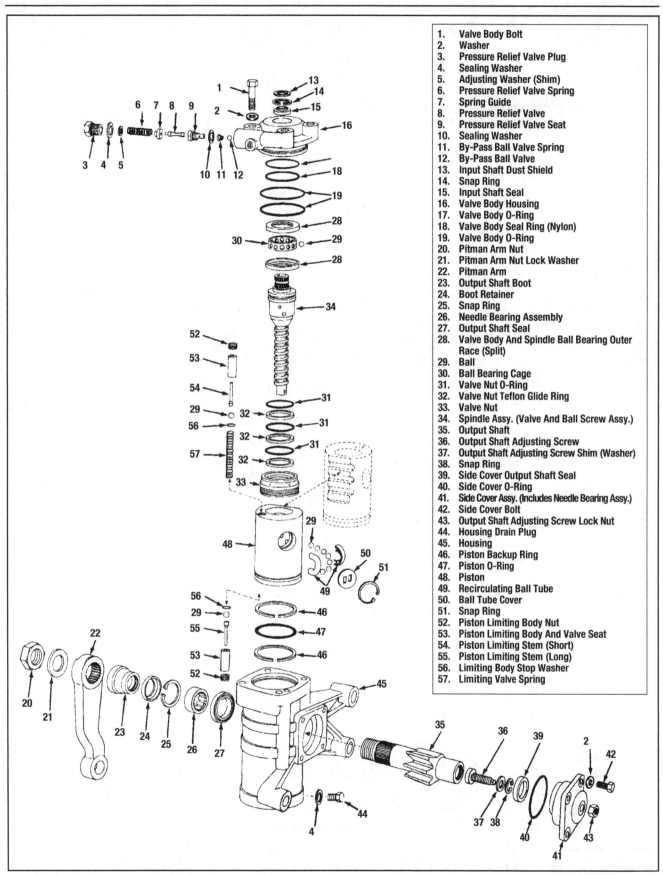

Exploded view of integral steering gear. *(Courtesy: Bendix Corp.)*

Steering System Diagnosis And Repair

system will cause the fluid to have a foamy appearance. If the pump is overheated, the fluid will become dark. Note that if the fluid does become discolored, other problems may exist in the power steering system. These might include a leak, allowing the reservoir to deplete itself of fluid, or a defective power steering cooler. In addition, dirt or water may have made its way into the reservoir, causing contamination.

If the problem is loss of power assist or inadequate power assist, be sure to check fluid level and belt tightness and condition before condemning the pump. The pump might actually be able to deliver full pressure under conditions when the steering isn't doing a lot of work, yet fail to provide enough flow to keep up with the driver's needs going into a sharp turn. If after checking the fluid level and condition and adjusting the belt tension, pump noises and/or lack of power steering assist are still present, replace the pump assembly.

Removal

Drain the power steering fluid from the pump reservoir and disconnect the power steering hoses from the pump. Loosen the belt tension (if equipped) and remove the belt from the pump pulley. If applicable, remove the pulley assembly for installation on the replacement pump. Disconnect the pump assembly from its mounting bracket(s). If the reservoir is integral with the pump, and is not supplied with the replacement pump, remove the reservoir as previously outlined.

NOTE: Most belt and gear driven pumps are rebuildable. Check with the pump manufacturer for specifications and instructions.

Installation

If applicable, install the pump reservoir onto the replacement pump using a new O-ring or gasket. Install the pump assembly to its mounting bracket(s), and torque the fasteners to manufacturer's specifications. Install the pump pulley and belt (if equipped), and adjust the belt to manufacturer's specifications. Reconnect the power steering hoses, being careful not to over-torque the pressure hose fitting.

Fill the reservoir with the specified power steering fluid and start the engine. Rotate the steering wheel from stop-to-stop, being careful not to hold the wheel against either stop for more than 2 seconds, to bleed the air from the system. Do not allow the reservoir to run dry of fluid. Inspect the fluid to ensure that there are no air bubbles.

POWER STEERING COOLER

A power steering cooler keeps the fluid temperature low, promoting longer component life and reducing the potential for leaks. A defective or blocked power steering cooler can contribute to heating the power steering fluid to the point that it could damage the rubber steering components, such as seals and hoses.

The cooler should be mounted in the engine compartment in an area that is exposed to an appropriate amount of air flow, such as the radiator area. As air passes through the cooler, heat from the fluid is dissipated into the atmosphere and the temperature of the fluid in the cooler is reduced.

Check to see if there is an adequate amount of fluid in the reservoir. Check the condition of the fluid, noting any discoloration. If the fluid has been overheated due to a defective cooler, it will be dark in color.

Replacement of the cooler involves disconnecting the power steering lines and removing the cooler from its mounting. Install the replacement cooler to its mounting and attach the power steering lines. Fill the system with the proper power steering fluid and bleed the air from the system. Start the engine and check for leaks.

POWER STEERING HOSES AND LINES

Warning: When the engine is running, the power steering fluid is under extreme pressure, which significantly raises its temperature. Injury can occur

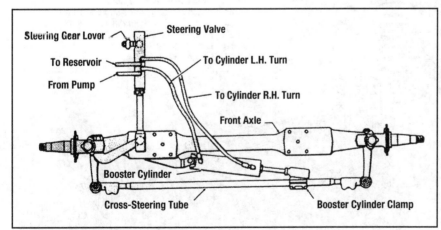

A spool valve controls high-pressure fluid routing to a power cylinder on vehicles with semi-integral power steering. The power cylinder piston assists the operator in turning the steering wheel by acting on the linkage.

Steering System Diagnosis And Repair

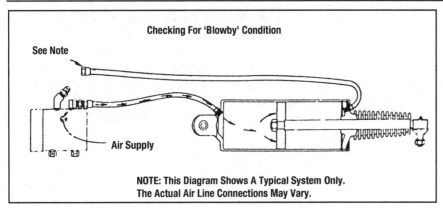

Testing for a piston blowby condition in the power cylinder of an air-assisted power steering unit.

STEERING WHEEL FREE-PLAY

Steering Wheel Diameter (in.)	Movement 45 degrees or (in.):
16	6 ¾ (17.1cm)
18	7 ⅛ (18.1cm)
19	7 ½ (19cm)
20	7 ⅞ (20cm)
21	8 ¼ (20.9cm)
22	8 ⅝ (21.9cm)

if adequate precautions are not followed.

Power steering hoses and lines carry hydraulic fluid throughout the system. The most common problem with power steering hoses and lines is leakage. Such leaks are a safety hazard for two reasons.

A power steering leak usually will mean the loss of steering assist. This will change the feel of the steering wheel and could cause an accident. The second hazard is fire. While power steering fluid is not itself readily flammable, it can burn easily when pressurized and sprayed in atomized form on a hot exhaust manifold.

When diagnosing a leak, clean the suspected area with an appropriate cleaning solution. Make sure the system has the correct amount of power steering fluid in the reservoir. Start the vehicle and rotate the steering wheel from stop-to-stop, being careful not to hold the wheel against either stop for more than 2 seconds.

Inspect hose fittings and clamps for tightness. If a fitting is found to be loose, remove the hose and check the hose fitting's O-ring seal. Make sure the seal is not damaged. Reinstall the hose and torque to manufacturer's specifications. If you find a loose hose clamp, tighten the clamp. Be careful not to tighten the clamp too much or hose damage may occur. If the clamp is damaged or will not tighten, replace it.

If you find leaky hoses that are cracked, hardened, deteriorated and mushy feeling or otherwise damaged, replacement is the only option. When hoses are replaced, the system should always be flushed to remove all debris that may have accumulated in the system.

POWER STEERING GEAR

There are two types of power steering gears: semi-integral and integral. With either semi-integral or integral power steering, the operator needs less effort to turn the steering wheel.

Semi-integral units provide hydraulic assistance to the steering unit with the use of a control valve, mounted in conjunction with a manual-type steering gear. Integral steering gear assemblies are self-contained hydraulic units, with the hydraulic pressure developed by an independently-mounted fluid pump driven by the engine.

A good starting point in troubleshooting a power steering gear is checking the performance of the system in terms of both operating smoothness and steering wheel play.

The following are the allowable steering wheel play (lash) maximums for power steering:

Begin checking the steering gear by feeling for and measuring the steering wheel free-play with the engine running, and the truck at a standstill. If there is excessive play, have an assistant turn the wheel slowly back and forth as you observe the operation of the linkages (engine on). Inspect all external steering linkage and the U-joint at the base of the steering column for looseness.

If any part of the system is binding, the linkage may cause difficult steering and make the driver suspect power steering hydraulic problems when the trouble is a simple, mechanical part of the steering system. If the binding seems to occur in the steering gear itself, it could be due to a worn or damaged bearing. If the gear has an adjustment for the sector shaft, adjust it to specification.

Next, perform a steering gear internal leakage test. The first step is to prevent operation of the gear's internal unloading valves. These may be a simple pressure relief valve or a valve located at either end of the steering gear piston's travel.

Have an assistant turn the steering wheel until the steering gear contacts the axle stops. Have him hold it there for just a few seconds while reading pressure and flow. The pressure should be at the pump relief pressure. Flow should be compared to factory specifications for gear leakage. If steering gear leakage is above acceptable levels, the steering gear should be overhauled or replaced.

Training for Certification 19

Steering System Diagnosis And Repair

Integral Gear

As the steering wheel is turned in either direction, a control valve directs the pressurized fluid against an end of the movable valve, which in turn causes the sector shaft to turn and move the steering linkage. When the steering wheel is moved in the opposite direction, the pressurized fluid is directed to the opposite side of the movable valve, causing the linkage to move in the opposite direction, changing the direction of the vehicle.

When overhauls are needed, perform them in accordance with the manufacturer's recommended procedures.

HYDRAULIC CYLINDER

Some steering systems use a hydraulic cylinder mounted on or with the steering linkage, which is actuated by the operation of the control valve when the steering gear is turned. The control pressure is developed by an independently mounted fluid pump driven by the engine. The control valve directs fluid under pressure to either side of the power piston within the cylinder in order to move the steering linkage either right or left. Various types are used, depending upon the linkage arrangement on the vehicle.

If the power cylinder is leaking, it should be replaced. However, if the steering displays a shimmy, the power cylinder could be loose at its bracket or not aligned properly with the steering linkage. Also, if the vehicle is displaying intermittent or no power assist, the power cylinder piston or rod could be binding. In these cases, replacement of the cylinder is warranted.

AIR ASSIST POWER CYLINDER

Some trucks are equipped with an air-assisted type of semi-integral unit. It is powered by the brake system's air compressor. The key component in the system is a torque valve, an integral part of a modified drag link (or in some cases a modified tie-rod) that replaces the original drag link. The torque valve senses more than 10-lbs. pressure on the wheel (0.04-in. movement) by changing its length very slightly. This, in turn, meters air to a power cylinder. The power cylinder is fastened to the frame and applies force to the wheel arm or tie-rod to assist the driver in turning and holding the steering linkage.

The air-assist safety valve should cut off steering assist when the dash mounted reservoir air pressure gauge drops to 60-65 psi. If the cutoff point is outside this range, adjust the valve as follows: Turn the hex socket set screw located in the center of the top cap of the safety valve. Turning the screw clockwise will raise the cutoff point; turning it counterclockwise will lower the cutoff point.

If this fails to correct the problem, clean the valve. Cleaning should be done every 100,000 miles as routine maintenance. To clean the air valve, remove it from the vehicle. Remove the capscrews retaining the valve cap and remove the valve cap from the valve body. Remove the spring cap, spring and air piston. Then, remove the O-ring from the piston.

Clean all parts in suitable solution. Inspect parts for wear, corrosion or damage. Replace the entire valve assembly if any wear, corrosion or damage is visible. Apply a thin coating of suitable lubricant and assemble the O-ring to the piston. Reassemble the spring cap, spring and air piston. Reinstall the valve onto the vehicle and check for proper operation and leakage.

To check the torque valve, make sure the entire system is lubricated. Build up brake system air pressure and shut down the engine. Listen for air leaks with the air valve in the neutral position (no torque on the steering wheel). There should be no leaks.

Keeping dirt out, disconnect the air lines at the torque valve and install pipe plugs. Have an assistant turn the steering wheel to extend and compress the valve about 1/16-in. in each direction, and listen for valve leaks. Some air will escape from the exhaust port when the valve first starts to feed as it begins to compress. Also, there may be a small burst of air when the wheel is turned in the opposite direction. However, air leakage should disappear as the assistant continues to extend or compress the valve through steering wheel action.

Replace the valve if it leaks. If there is a steering problem and the safety valve and torque valve are OK, check the power cylinder.

To check the power cylinder, make sure it is properly adjusted and does not bind as the wheels are turned. The line going to the port opposite the rotating end should be connected, but the other air line should be disconnected. Make sure air system pressure is built up all the way and the engine is off. Raise and safely support the vehicle so that the wheels are off the floor.

Have an assistant turn the steering wheel in the direction that will cause the torque valve to extend. Listen at the end of the disconnected hose. If a substantial quantity of air escapes, the power cylinder piston is worn.

Connect the disconnected hose to the torque valve. Disconnect the hose that is connected. Have the assistant turn the wheels in the opposite direction. If a substantial quantity of air escapes, the power cylinder piston is worn.

Replacement of the power cylinder consists of draining the system of hydraulic fluid (or air as the case may be), disconnecting the lines and removing the cylinder from

Steering System Diagnosis And Repair

the linkage and frame mounting.

Steering Gear Removal

With the wheels in the straight-ahead position, mark the steering column coupler and the steering gear input shaft for assembly reference. Mark and remove the steering gear fluid lines, and drain the hydraulic fluid. Remove the cotter pin (if equipped) and securing nut that attaches the pitman arm to the steering linkage. Using a suitable puller, disconnect the pitman arm from the steering linkage. Remove the steering gear bolts and the steering gear assembly (with the pitman arm still attached).

DISASSEMBLY

NOTE: These procedures pertain to Bendix™ integral steering gears, and are intended to give you a basic overview of steering gear service. Model-specific overhaul procedures, special tool usage, specifications and tolerances will vary depending on the particular steering gear manufacturer.

Clean the power steering gear with a suitable solution and secure it in a vise with soft jaw protectors, being careful not to over-tighten the vise. Remove the drain plug from the housing and drain the hydraulic fluid. Separate the valve body from the housing assembly by removing the fasteners and rotating the output shaft with the pitman arm. Continue to withdraw the valve body from the housing.

Remove the pitman arm nut, mark the pitman arm in relation to the output shaft, and using a suitable puller, remove the pitman arm. Do not use heat or pound on the pitman arm or output shaft as damage can result. Remove any dirt or foreign debris from the exposed portion of the output shaft.

Loosen and remove the adjusting screw locknut, and remove the side cover bolts. Turn the head of the adjusting screw clockwise, lifting the side cover from the housing. Install the pitman arm, and use it to center the piston and output shaft sector teeth inside the cover opening. Remove the pitman arm and remove the output shaft by gently tapping on the splined end with a soft-headed mallet.

Prevent the input shaft from rotating and remove the ball screw, valve body, and piston from the housing. Remove the O-rings and backup rings from the piston groove. Remove the retaining ring and tube cover. Lift out both halves of the ball return tube. Rotate the input shaft and ball screw counterclockwise to remove the remainder of the internal balls. Separate the piston from the ball screw. Mark the limiting valve stems for assembly reference.

NOTE: These stems must be installed in the same end of the piston from which they are removed.

Remove the limiting body nut, body stem, ball valve, stop washer and spring. Remove the limiting body nut and washer from the opposite end of the piston. Remove the rubber boot, retainer and seal from the housing assembly. Remove the retainer, O-ring and bearing.

NOTE: It is not necessary to remove the outer bearing race if it is in good condition. If the outer race is worn, damaged or otherwise not reusable, the side cover and outer race must be replaced as an assembly.

Remove the valve nut and the ball screw assembly, ball race, ball cage and bearings. Remove the O-rings and inner ball race from the valve body, and the retaining ring and seal. The valve body has pressure relief and safety valves. Remove the plug and its corresponding washer.

NOTE: Pressure adjusting shims are located in the plug. Reinstalling these shims properly is critical in maintaining the correct relief pressure.

Remove the spring, guide and valve. Loosen and remove the body and its seal washer as well as the spring and ball of the bypass valve. Remove the retaining ring adjustment screw spacer and adjusting screw from the output shaft.

CLEANING AND INSPECTION

Clean all parts individually in a suitable solution, and let them dry thoroughly. Replace all non-metallic parts. Carefully inspect all parts, especially the bearings, races, sector gear and piston teeth, input and output shafts, ball screw exterior, and the interior and exterior of the piston housing bore.

Minor scuffing of the exterior of the piston and housing bore is acceptable. Replace the parts if deep scoring is detected. Failure to do so will result in leakage and/or lack of steering control and reaction. Do not attempt to hone or bore these parts.

ASSEMBLY

Secure the valve body in a vise with soft jaw protectors. Install the ball, spring, valve seat and seal washer. Torque to manufacturer's specifications. Install the relief valve rod, guide and corresponding spring. Place a seal washer onto the plug with the adjusting shims and torque to manufacturer's specifications.

Install the seal and retaining ring into the valve body. Install the inner ball race into the bottom of the valve body and install the O-rings. Install the cage on the ball screw. Install the outer ball race and, using suitable grease to hold them in place, insert the new bearing balls. Insert the entire assembly into the valve body.

Replace the glide seal rings and O-rings, using a seal protector to seat them. Without removing the tool, insert the nut into the valve body and screw in by hand until the tool backs itself out. Torque the valve nut to manufacturer's specifications.

Install the stop washer, limiting valve stem and limiting body in the appropriate end of the piston. Apply a small amount of Loctite™ on the threads of the limiting body nuts and install in the piston. Torque to manufacturer's specifications.

Install the ball valve, spring, stop washer and limiting body on the other end of the piston. Apply a small amount of Loctite™ on the threads of the limiting body nut. Install the nut in the piston, and torque to manufacturer's specifications.

NOTE: As stated earlier, the limiting valve stems must be installed in the same end of the piston from which they were removed. The shortest stem should be installed in the end of the piston that contains the opening for the spindle assembly.

Install the spindle assembly into the piston, leaving approximately 1-in. between the valve body and piston. Insert the new balls one by one into the right recirculating tube hole of the piston. Rotate the input shaft counterclockwise as the balls are inserted, until they appear at the opening at the other end of the recirculating tube. Make sure the balls are at an equal depth in both of the holes. This ensures correct installation of the return tube.

CAUTION: Extreme care must be taken when performing these steps. If this group is somehow installed incorrectly, the result may be one or more balls falling inside the piston or coming out at the top and lodging in the bottom of the housing.

If the entire bearing assembly, outer race and bearing spacers were removed, install the thick bearing spacer onto a suitable seal installation tool, making sure the flat side of the spacer rests against the large diameter of the tool. Insert the tool through the side cover opening of the housing, making sure the spacer is square in its bore. Tap the spacer approximately 1/8 to 3/16 inch into the bore using a soft-headed mallet. Center the narrow bearing spacer on the race installation tool, and drive the bearing and race along with the spacer into the housing from the output shaft side of the housing, until the tool bottoms out on the outside of the housing.

Remove the tool and check that the outer race and spacer has been driven through the housing sufficiently to allow installation of the retaining ring. Install the seal onto the tool so the lip groove rests against the large diameter of the tool. Insert the tool through the side cover opening of the housing, and use a soft-headed mallet to drive the seal into place.

Install the boot retainer into the housing, and install the small diameter of the boot into the retainer, making sure it is seated properly within the groove formed by the retainer. Install the valve body, spindle and piston into the housing, being careful not to damage the O-rings. Install the valve body bolts and washers and torque to manufacturer's specifications.

Rotate the input shaft to center the piston teeth in the side cover opening, to facilitate installation of the output shaft, allowing proper mesh between the sector and piston teeth. Install the adjusting screw spacer and retaining ring into the output shaft.

NOTE: Spacer thickness is to be selected so the axial play of the adjusting screw is within manufacturer's specifications after the retaining ring is installed.

Insert the roller bearing into the side cover. Install the side cover seal onto a suitable seal instillation tool so the lip groove rests against the large diameter of the tool. Install the thick bearing spacer onto the tool, making sure the flat side of the spacer rests against the seal. Insert the tool and install the seal ring into its groove on the side cover.

Pack the output shaft bearings in the side cover and housing with suitable grease, and lubricate the seals in the side cover and housing using the same grease. Install the side cover onto the output shaft, and torque the adjusting screw to manufacturer's specifications.

Before inserting the output shaft into the housing, wrap a single layer of masking tape around the splines and threads to protect the housing seal during installation. Lubricate the exterior of the tape with a suitable lubricant. Install the housing with a twisting motion. Install the housing washers and bolts and torque to manufacturer's specifications.

Steering Gear Installation

Install the steering gear to the vehicle frame and torque the bolts to manufacturer's specifications. Install the pitman arm onto the steering gear output shaft, aligning the marks made during removal. Install the pitman arm output shaft nut and torque to manufacturer's

Steering System Diagnosis And Repair

specifications. Install the securing nut that attaches the pitman arm to the steering linkage, and torque to manufacturer's specifications while aligning the nut castellation to the cotter pin holes (if equipped). Install the cotter pin.

Reconnect the steering gear fluid lines. Reconnect the steering column at the input shaft, aligning the marks made during removal. Test the power steering system for pressure and flow values, and check for leaks.

Relief Valve Plunger Adjustment

These valves reduce the steering pressure when the road wheels reach their limits in a turn, so the steering pump will not operate at maximum pressure. They should be reset after an overhaul or whenever they have been replaced. They can also be reset according to the manufacturer's recommendations, when the axle stops need to be reset; i.e., when large tires have been installed.

To adjust, first have the engine at idle and put normal weight on the front axle. Then, have an assistant turn the wheel all the way in one direction until you hear a high-pressure hiss or the axle stop is contacted.

Turn the relief valve for that direction in or out and have the helper repeatedly approach the stop slowly until the hiss can be heard when there is 3/8- to 3/16-in. clearance at the axle stop. Repeat this procedure in the other direction.

STEERING LINKAGE

When the steering wheel is rotated in either direction, the steering gear transfers motion from the output shaft to the pitman arm. The pitman arm is splined and mounted to the steering gear sector (or output) shaft. The other end of the pitman arm is connected to the drag link or relay arm. The drag link or relay arm transfers the pitman arm motion to the tie-rods, and then to the steering arms. The steering arms are part of, or attached to the steering knuckle spindles. When the steering linkage is moved, the steering knuckle rotates on the suspension arm ball joints or kingpins.

You may be able to detect steering linkage that operates roughly or loosely from underneath if part of the system obviously operates in an uneven manner. When the linkage is suspected of binding, or of being too loose, the technician should disconnect it from other parts of the steering system, raise the front axle off the floor and support it in a safe manner. Then rotate the part slowly by hand in order to feel for binding or looseness.

The steering linkage can also be inspected using a procedure called a 'dry park check'. With the engine off, have an assistant rotate the steering wheel from side-to-side while you inspect the steering linkage joints for looseness. Any side-to-side movement of the steering linkage joints is cause for replacement.

Pitman Arm

The pitman arm is the strongest component in the steering linkage system. It is made of steel and designed to accept the turning motion of the steering gear output shaft. It then transfers that motion into the torque needed to move the rest of the steering linkage back-and-forth. The pitman arm is splined to the steering gear output shaft and secured to the shaft by a large nut.

Removal

Remove the cotter pin (if equipped) from the nut that secures the pitman arm to the steering linkage, and remove the securing nut. Position the front wheels in the straight-ahead position. Using a suitable puller, disconnect the steering linkage from the pitman arm.

Mark the pitman arm in relation to the output shaft for assembly reference. Remove the pitman arm attaching nut and washer. Using a suitable puller, extract the pitman arm from the steering gear output shaft.

Installation

With the front wheels in the straight-ahead position, place the pitman arm on the steering gear output shaft, aligning the marks made during removal. Install the washer and nut and torque to manufacturer's specifications.

Install the steering linkage and the securing nut that attaches the pitman arm to the linkage, then torque the securing nut to manufacturer's specifications while aligning the castellation of the nut to the cotter pin holes (if equipped). Install the cotter pin.

Drag Link/Relay Rod

The drag link or relay rod is made of forged steel. It secures the pitman arm to the steering arm, and is sometimes adjustable, depending on its configuration.

Removal

Raise and safely support the vehicle. Remove the cotter pins (if equipped) and nuts that attach the drag link to the steering linkage. Disconnect the drag link from the steering linkage using a suitable puller.

Installation

Install the drag link onto the steering linkage. Install the attaching nuts and torque to manufacturer's specifications, while aligning the nut castellation to the cotter

Steering System Diagnosis And Repair

pin holes (if equipped). Install the cotter pin.

Tie-Rod Assembly

Removal

Raise and safely support the vehicle. Remove the wheel. Remove the cotter pin (if equipped) and remove the tie-rod end nut. Pull the tie-rod end from the steering arm or knuckle arm using a suitable puller.

Loosen the clamping bolt and unscrew the tie-rod end from the tie-rod sleeve assembly. Count the number of turns required to remove the tie-rod end for assembly reference. Inspect the clamping bolt and clamp for damage and replace as necessary.

Installation

Screw the tie-rod end into the tie-rod sleeve assembly the same number of turns referenced during removal. Torque the clamping nut to manufacturer's specifications.

Install the tie-rod end onto the steering arm or knuckle arm. Install the attaching nut and torque to manufacturer's specifications, while aligning the nut castellation to the cotter pin holes (if equipped). Install the cotter pin.

Steering Arm

Removal

Raise and safely support the vehicle. Remove the wheel and drum or rotor. Remove the cotter pin (if equipped) and remove the tie-rod end nut. Pull the tie-rod end from the steering arm or knuckle arm using a suitable puller. Unbolt the steering arm and remove it from the spindle assembly.

Installation

Secure the steering arm to the spindle assembly and torque the bolts or nut to manufacturer's specifications. Install the tie-rod end onto the steering arm. Install the attaching nut and torque to manufacturer's specifications, while aligning the nut castellation to the cotter pin holes (if equipped). Install the cotter pin.

Notes

Suspension System Diagnosis And Repair

Any suspension is a system. That means each part affects every other. With leaf springs, this is an especially important point. In practice, it means that the part that fails is only a symptom, not the disease. You have to look further for what actually caused the failure.

Regular lubrication is absolutely critical to the life of all components, not just bushings. Any time a suspension component begins to develop friction or even become seized (which of course results frequently when parts are not lubed regularly), stresses are imposed that are almost sure to break other parts. Also, breakage of spring parts often results from looseness. The problem can only be properly repaired if all the spring leaves that are broken, and retaining parts, such as the top plate and U-bolts that were affected, are replaced.

DIAGNOSIS

When the vehicle is experiencing a wander or weave, look for:
- Tire pressure incorrect
- Tires of unequal size or improper type
- Tires unevenly worn
- Wheel lugnuts loose
- Bent spindle
- Wheel bearings loose or worn
- Kingpins worn or bent
- Kingpins tight in steering knuckles or bushings
- Steering gear assembly too tight or too loose
- Improper alignment
- Front axle bent or shifted (worn suspension parts)
- Springs broken
- Frame diamond-shaped
- Rear axle housing shifted or bent
- Steering linkage tight or binding
- Drag link is of the wrong length (wrong part), causing steering gear to operate off-center
- Lack of lubrication to front suspension or steering linkage causing wear and looseness
- Defective power steering assembly
- Tractor-trailer fifth wheel damaged or galled, poorly lubricated or improperly positioned.

If the suspension exhibits excessive harshness when driving, look for:
- Improper tire pressure
- Springs broken, causing binding between leaves or reduced flexing
- Springs too stiff (spring weight rating is much higher than required)
- Shock absorbers too stiff or malfunctioning
- Front-end alignment incorrect
- Loose suspension components
- Air suspension-ride height incorrectly adjusted
- Seized spring shackles.

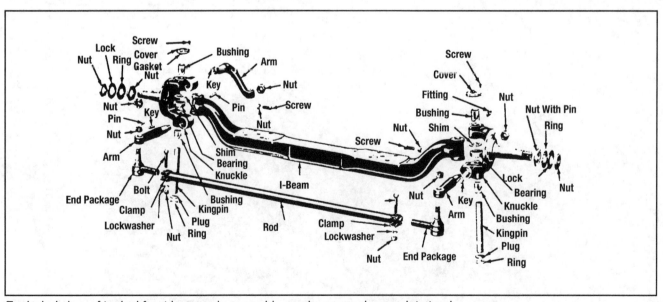

Exploded view of typical front beam axle assembly used on many heavy-duty trucks.

Suspension System Diagnosis And Repair

If the suspension or steering is noisy, look for:
- Lack of, or improper, lubrication
- Loose steering linkage
- Loose suspension parts
- Loose brake parts
- Worn universal
- Worn differential
- Loose sheet metal.

FRONT AXLE ASSEMBLY

The front axles used on heavy-duty trucks are rated by their load carrying capacity; and the greater the load, the bigger the axle. The axles are forged and then machined in various places to accept the springs and the steering knuckles. The springs are retained to the axle by U-bolts while kingpins hold the steering knuckles in place. The kingpins are held to the axle by either one or two tapered draw pins.

Steering arms are bolted to or are a part of the steering knuckle and are connected to the steering linkage. The steering knuckles rotate on the kingpins as the steering linkage is moved by the steering mechanism.

Front axles on many trucks have been moved slightly to the rear (or set back) as regulations regarding overall truck length have changed. While axles almost always were forward of the engine oil pan in the past, many trucks now locate the pan forward of the axle. This has provided longer, smoother riding springs and improved front tire life. The latter has happened because those tires are more consistently loaded and less likely to develop uneven tread wear. In some cases, the longer springs and softer ride make it more important to maintain the performance of shock absorbers.

Removal

Raise and safely support the vehicle. Remove the front wheels. If equipped with air brakes, completely drain the system and disconnect the air lines. If equipped with hydraulic brakes, disconnect the hydraulic lines. If equipped with drum brakes, remove the hub and drum assembly. Remove the anchor plate with the entire brake assembly attached. If equipped with disc brakes, remove the brake calipers and disc rotors.

Remove the shock absorbers and the stabilizer bar (if equipped). Disconnect the tie-rod ends and remove the steering knuckles. Place a suitable floor jack under the center of the axle and remove the nuts from the U-bolts. Carefully lower the axle away from the springs.

Installation

Jack the axle into position, making sure the alignment lugs correctly engage the springs and mounting plates. Install new U-bolts and torque using the manufacturer's procedures and specifications. Install the steering knuckles and connect the tie-rod ends. Install the stabilizer bar (if equipped) and shock absorbers.

If equipped with disc brakes, install the disc rotors and calipers. If equipped with drum brakes, install the brake assemblies, drums, and hub assemblies. Reconnect all brake lines. If equipped with hydraulic brakes, bleed the system. Reinstall the front wheels and check vehicle alignment.

KINGPINS

The kingpin secures the steering knuckle to the axle. It can be either tapered or straight, depending on the manufacturer. Inspection and lubrication of the kingpin must be performed in accordance with the manufacturer's recommended service procedures.

Many sizes of kingpins and bushings are used, but most are basic in their design. The kingpins, bushings and thrust bearings can be replaced without removing the axle assembly from the truck. Kingpins and bushings especially, are critical wear parts that must be replaced regularly if the truck's alignment is to remain true.

Raise and safely support the front end of the truck so the wheels clear the floor. Make sure the wheel bearings are properly adjusted. Apply the brakes to ensure that the front wheels are locked.

Install a camber gauge according to the manufacturer's instructions. Attempt to move the tire in-and-out while looking at the kingpin bushings. Check the camber change, and if it exceeds the manufacturer's specifications, replace the kingpin.

NOTE: Lubricating the kingpins will help eliminate some play, but this is only a temporary remedy.

When checking for excessive kingpin wear, also check for:
- Worn, cracked, misaligned or missing seals and gaskets
- Damage due to the use of high levels of road salt
- Misaligned seals, bearings, shims, bushings or draw keys
- Incorrect lubricant being used
- Lubrication interval inadequate either according to basic schedule or the need to lubricate more often in the particular application
- Lubrication not being applied properly (with weight off wheels, etc.)
- Knuckle bore out-of-round, distorting knuckle bushings.

Removal

Raise and safely support the vehicle. Remove the front wheels. If equipped with air brakes, completely drain the system and disconnect the air lines. If equipped with hydraulic brakes, disconnect

Suspension System Diagnosis And Repair

the hydraulic lines.

If equipped with drum brakes, remove the hub and drum assembly. Remove the anchor plate with the entire brake assembly attached. If equipped with disc brakes, remove the brake calipers and disc rotors. Disconnect the steering arms from the spindle, and remove the bolts that attach the upper and lower dust cap and gasket to the spindle.

On threaded key applications, back off the draw key nuts and gently strike the nut with a brass hammer to loosen the key. Remove the nut and drive the draw key out with a suitable drift. On staked draw key applications, drive the staked draw key out at the opposite end of the staking, using a suitable drift and a brass hammer.

With the axle assembly supported, drive the kingpin downward using a suitable drift and hammer. Remove the spindle, thrust bearing assembly and shims from the axle center. Press the bushings from the spindle bores using a suitable press.

Measure the kingpin bores. If the bore in the axle is not within manufacturer's specifications, the bore must be reamed to allow installation of an oversized kingpin. If oversized kingpins are not an option, the axle must be replaced.

Installation

Press the bushings into the spindle bores using a suitable press. Place the spindle on the axle center end and support it. Slide the thrust bearing between the lower face of the axle center and the steering knuckle lower yoke.

Align the kingpin holes in the spindle yoke with the kingpin hole in the axle center. Raise the spindle to take up the clearance between the lower yoke, thrust bearing and lower face of the axle center end.

Align the flats on the kingpin to align with the draw key holes in the axle center. Drive the kingpin into the spindle from the top down until the draw key holes are aligned. Install the draw key and tap it with a hammer to seat it. At the bottom

Tapered kingpin design contains spindle clearance adjustments provided by a taper nut in the upper spindle cover. A locknut and cotter key prevent severe road vibrations from loosening or altering the settings.

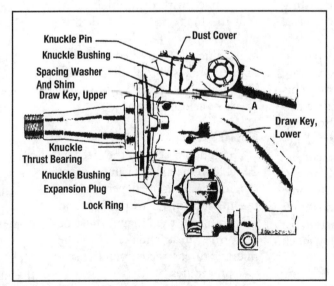

Cross section of a steering knuckle assembly using a straight kingpin. Draw keys retain the kingpin and prevent rotation of the pin in the axle beam.

of the spindle, install the expansion plug and the retainer ring.

Install the steering arm and all brake components that were removed. Clean, inspect, and repack the wheel bearings, and install the hub and wheel. Bleed the brakes (if necessary).

SHOCK ABSORBERS

Shock absorbers dampen energy from the suspension system by converting that energy into heat. This energy would otherwise become stored in the springs, causing maximum stresses throughout the suspension system. Also, acting as a downstop for severe suspension bottoming, the shocks protect the springs from overload and breakage.

Worn shocks can be a major cause of uneven tire wear. They can cause body sway in turns or cross winds, rough ride, and reduced traction due to uncontrolled wheel jounce. When there is no shock dampening, the truck tends to ride up and down at the natural frequency of the springs.

Shock absorbers contain hydraulic fluid or gas, along with pistons and seals in a cylinder. Up and down motion forces the fluid or gas back and forth through a valve inside the shock housing. The energy that would otherwise perpetuate the jounce is converted to heat through friction. In this way, the spring is kept relatively near the center of its travel where its supporting force is more in line

Suspension System Diagnosis And Repair

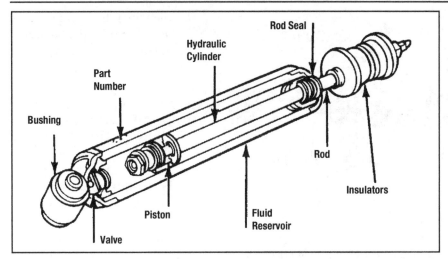

Cross-sectional view of a typical shock absorber. *(Courtesy: Ford Motor Co.)*

with the vehicle weight. Thus, the harshness is taken out of the suspension's operation.

A good way to test shock absorbers is to drive the truck a considerable distance (say 5 to 10 miles) over relatively irregular road surfaces and then quickly check their temperature with your hand. A shock that's working will be noticeably above the outside temperature.

If you're unsure about the temperature, disconnect the shock at one end and attempt to compress it by hand. You should feel a strong resistance. Also, the after the shock is compressed, it should return to its fully-extended position. Inspect shock brackets for cracks or breaks that may cause good shocks to become ineffective. Look for hydraulic leaks, which most often occur around the piston rods.

Removal

In most cases, the vehicle does not have to be raised to replace the shock absorbers. Remove the retaining nuts and washers on both the upper and lower flanges. It is important to make sure that the bushings come off with the shock absorber. Remove the shock absorber and inspect the mounting flanges for damage.

Installation

Install the shock absorber with new bushings onto the mounting flanges. Install the retaining nuts and washers and torque to manufacturer's specifications. Shock absorbers should be replaced in pairs for the particular axle.

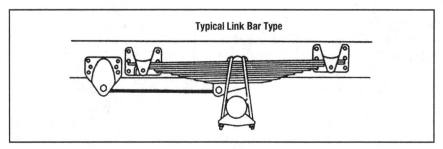

Link bar suspension counteracts the tendency of the drive axle to distort the spring due to torque reactions and helps to maintain proper axle alignment position.

LEAF SPRINGS

Leaf-type springs are used to support and cushion the chassis and load weight from the road or off-road surface. The springs are usually multi-leaf, one- or two-stage types or tapered two or three leaf types. When the one- or two-stage types are used, the first stage provides a soft ride when the vehicle is empty and the second stage provides additional support when the vehicle is loaded. The tapered leaf springs are normally used when a known constant weight is to be supported. The tapered leaf springs are all full length while the stage-type springs vary in length.

The spring has a progressive rate of supporting force, so that the more it is bent as the vehicle moves up-and-down, the greater its resistance. The spring must be allowed to flex and this is accomplished by having one

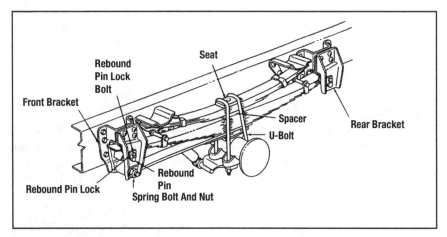

A typical variable-rate rear spring installation in a single-axle vehicle. Under light loads, the vehicle is sprung for the lower leaf assembly only. As greater loads are placed on the unit, the upper portion will add supporting strength.

Suspension System Diagnosis And Repair

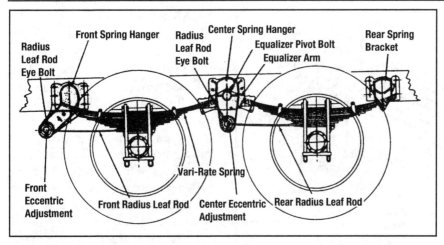

A typical rear tandem axle with link bar installation. This arrangement uses center fixed eyebolts with sliding box spring brackets at the front and rear to allow spring length changes.

end, normally the rear, free to move by a shackle arrangement or by having the end free to slide back and forth as the spring flexes.

Rubber bushings are normally used as insulators between the spring eye bolts and the frame mounts. A centering bolt is used through the spring leaves to keep the leaves together and to mate with a hole in the axle to properly position the spring. U-bolts are used to bolt the spring to the axle.

With rear suspensions, different leaf spring arrangements are used depending upon the expected load to be carried and the number of axles needed to support the load. The most common leaf spring arrangement is the variable-rate spring with an auxiliary spring mounted to the top to give greater support under periods of heavy loads. This type of spring is normally used on the single axle arrangement.

When leaf springs are used with tandem axles, they can be mounted directly over each axle, or mounted between the axles and the axles connected to each other by one equalizing beam on each side.

Another way of explaining this is to say that rear leaf spring suspensions are divided into two basic categories: Single- and dual-point. Single-point types use a beam that has bushings on both ends. The spring uses front and rear hangers. Torque rods locate the axles laterally. Dual-point types have four springs instead of two. An equalizer allows a degree of articulation between the axles in some designs.

There may also be torque rods (one for each of the four spring packs) in order to minimize the need for the springs to handle acceleration and braking torque. Other tandem suspensions, designed for super-heavy loads and mostly off-road usage, are mounted on rubber blocks and use no leaf springs.

The following are recommendations for keeping spring suspension systems performing at their best:

- Whenever one spring leaf is broken, all the others have been overloaded, and running under increased stress. Keep a watchful eye for broken leaves and replace them as soon as possible. If there is any reason to believe a truck has run with one or more broken leaves for a length of time, replace the entire set. Whenever two leaves have broken, replace the entire set due to the stresses placed on the remaining springs.
- When a single leaf of a set of long, front springs breaks, it is probably worthwhile to replace the entire set; there are fewer leaves in these types of suspensions, and flexing is very great.
- Never reuse U-bolts because of the stretching that occurs during normal initial torque, and the impossibility of getting effective clamping force or pull-up torque when they are retorqued.
- One broken or worn part can destroy a suspension system. So, whenever a failure or problem occurs, don't just replace the bad parts; inspect and replace the parts related to the one(s) that failed.

The first thing the technician must understand is that there is almost no tolerance for movement between the leaves in the center section. The force of movement will pull and tear the spring and spring saddle if the system is not properly installed and maintained.

If the top plate is worn, bent or cracked, the plate won't seat flat against the top of the top spring. When these parts move against each other, the result is premature failure. If the plate is made of cast iron, you'll probably see the problem. If it is made of steel or forged, it will often not be brittle enough to break, but could be dished. Using a plate that is dished is hazardous because the plate aligns the U-bolt; and when the plate is dished, the bolt will be misaligned. Don't fabricate a plain steel block plate because the precision holes drilled in the original equipment plate are necessary to maintain alignment.

After the spring stack has settled, the spring will compress. The reduced thickness causes the retention parts to loosen, resulting in movement that creates wear and, ultimately, failure. It's important to note that stack settling is a normal wear process that must be dealt with by proper maintenance.

It may be appropriate to replace individual broken spring leaves under some conditions, while in others it will probably pay the user to replace the entire pack once a failure occurs in any of the leaves.

When experiencing chronic spring breakage at low mileage, look for:

- Failure to retorque new U-bolts at specified mileage intervals
- Failure to replace U-bolts after disassembly or replacement with a bolt of improper rating
- Seized spring shackles
- Worn hangers, bushings or spring pins
- Failure to replace individual broken leaves shortly after they fail
- Overloading
- Heavy loads in combination with shock loads (driver races over railroad tracks or rough roads with heavy loads — spring typically breaks with a jagged edge)
- Worn torque rods
- Spring excessively hardened (if spring breaks clean)
- Spring bends when truck has not been overloaded - spring inadequately hardened in manufacturing.

Removal

Raise and safely support the vehicle at the frame. Raise the axle so the tires clear the floor. Disconnect the stabilizer bar (if equipped), and remove the torque rods (if equipped). Place a floor jack underneath the axle assembly and remove the lower shock absorber mounts. Remove the U-bolt nuts and then remove the front and rear spring retainer bolts. Remove the U-bolts and seats and lower the axle/spring assembly using the floor jack.

Inspection

Clean the springs using a steam cleaner or suitable cleaning solution. Inspect the assembly and replace all leaves that are cracked or broken. Inspect the arc of the leaves, replacing any leaves that are flattened out. Inspect the spring pins and shackles (if equipped) for damage. Check for damaged or worn spring eye or shackle bushings. Inspect the spring shackle mounting bolts and brackets for damage.

Disassembly

CAUTION: Never use heat to disassemble any suspension part, as it will weaken the metal.

Using a vise, secure one end of the spring assembly and remove the spring eye bushing. Reposition the spring in the vise so that it is secured in the center of the spring. Remove the rebound clips. Remove the center bolt and carefully open the vise, allowing the leaves to spread apart. Note the spring assembly order and remove the leaves from the center bolt.

Assembly

Using suitable grease, lightly lubricate the spring leaves. Align the center bolt hole using a drift and assemble the leaves in the reverse order of removal.

Secure the spring in the vise and compress it to allow installation of the center bolt. Install a new center bolt through the spring leaves and install the center bolt nut. Do not torque to specification at this time.

NOTE: It is important to always replace the center bolt when rebuilding a spring assembly.

Install a suitable clamping tool to hold the spring leaves in alignment during assembly. Install the spring leaf rebound clips. Torque the center bolt nut to manufacturer's specifications and remove the clamping tool. Reposition the spring assembly so that the end of the spring is in the vise, and install a new spring eye bushing.

Installation

NOTE: Replace the leaf spring U-bolts and nuts whenever a spring is removed.

Mount the pivot end of the spring into the frame bracket and install the spring pin and roller. Align the opposite end of the spring with the bracket or shackle and install the spring pin and roller. If the spring pins are secured with nuts, torque to manufacturer's specifications.

Secure the axle assembly to the spring by installing the U-bolt upper and lower seats along with their U-bolts and nuts. Tighten the U-bolts securely, but do not torque to specification at this time. Install the stabilizer bar (if equipped), and the torque rods (if equipped). Lower the vehicle so that its weight is fully on the spring.

U-Bolt Torque

After replacing spring leaves, the top plate or U-bolts, follow the manufacturer's torquing recommendations. Some manufacturers recommend retorquing with the spring under load after 5-10 miles of driving and again after 500-1,000 miles. Retorquing at the required intervals is the only way of ensuring reliable service and optimum component life.

The spring stack will often feel solid even if clamping force is too weak to do the job. You can get a fairly good indication of proper clamping force if you rap the U-bolt with a brass hammer. If the

Suspension System Diagnosis And Repair

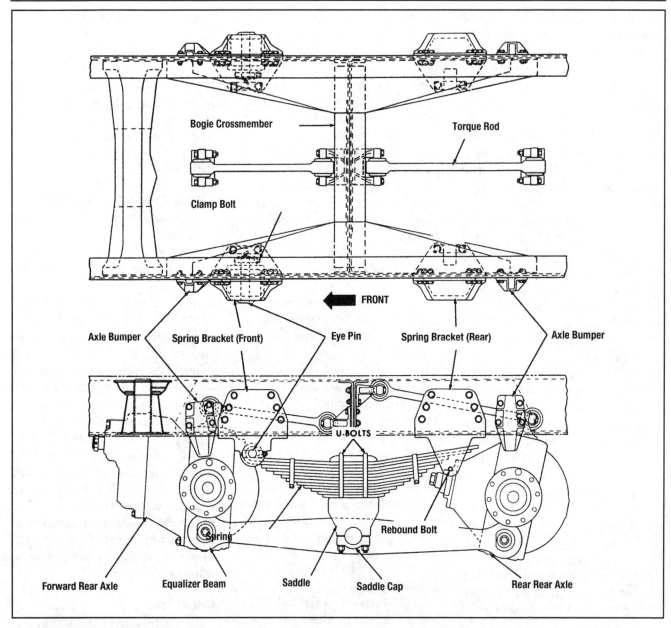

Hendrickson suspension for a tandem rear axle vehicle uses two torque rods, and an equalizing beam and spring saddle, so only one spring per side can be used to support the vehicle and load

sound you get is a dull thud, it isn't clamping properly, regardless of pull-around torque. If the sound you get is a ringing sound, the bolt is probably clamping effectively.

It is also important to heed manufacturer's recommendations as to U-bolt replacement and grade. It is strongly recommended to replace the bolt every time the stack is disassembled for repair. The reason is that the bolt, during normal, correct torquing, is stretched past what is called its elastic limit. That means the bolt is permanently lengthened just a little to get more torque. Proper torquing, however, does not take the bolt to its yield point, where it suddenly starts to lose its strength.

Note that the Society of Automotive Engineers' (SAE) grade of bolt is critical. Some manufacturers recommend at least a Grade 7 bolt (115,000 psi yield strength) for highway trucks and Grade 8 (130,000 psi) for off-road. Obviously, a bolt that yields at a lower stretching force will not only fail to apply adequate clamping force to the system when assembled, but will not maintain effective clamping force. Also, overtorquing will fail to correct a problem because that will weaken the bolt and guarantee that it cannot maintain tension.

A U-bolt should always be replaced after it has been disassembled because the torquing process has changed its stretch characteristics and also changed the distance

Suspension System Diagnosis And Repair

between threads. These facts, together with the natural tendency for the bolt to develop rust and scale on the threads, add up to one basic problem with reusing a bolt: Even if the rotating or pull-around torque applied is correct, the torque the bolt applies to the assembly (pull-up torque) will not be.

TORQUE ARMS

When a truck is equipped with tandem axles, torque arms are normally used to maintain or adjust the alignment of the axles to each other and to the frame. The torque arms can be located on each side of the frame.

Torque arms keep the axle from twisting under the chassis in reaction to the torque load from the drivetrain. Movement from side-to-side due to worn torque rod parts will overload the suspension system, resulting in premature wear or even failure of parts.

For that reason, running with worn torque arms will ruin a good spring repair job and will affect the drivetrain in such areas as differential seals, the axle housings and gears. It will also result in premature tire wear. A torque arm that has moved 1/8-in. from its original position should be replaced. Bad bushings or elongated holes are also indications that replacement is necessary.

Removal

Disconnect the torque arms from the axle assembly and the frame mount. Note the position and number of alignment spacers (if equipped). Inspect the axle bracket boss for excessive wear, and replace if necessary.

Installation

Install the torque arms, being sure to use the correct length for the vehicle. Connect the end to the frame side rail first and the end to the axle next. Torque the securing bolts or nuts to manufacturer's specifications.

EQUALIZING BEAMS

Equalizing beam suspension systems assist in the articulation of tandem axles, especially when driving on uneven surfaces. They do what their name implies; they equalize the load and distribute weight evenly between both axles.

Lubrication of the bushings on which the beams ride is important. Also, fasteners must be kept tight to maintain clamping force between the inside surface of the axle bracket legs and the shoulders of the steel ball.

There should be no motion between the steel ball and through-shaft or axle bracket legs, or between the bronze socket and beam end-hub. Torque of through-shaft nuts should be checked periodically and kept to specification.

Beam end-connection fasteners should be torqued after a repair and then periodically retorqued.

Beam end-bushings should be checked periodically by placing a jack under the beam end to check for movement of the rubber end bushing inner metal. If there is movement, replace the end bushing and all connecting parts, rather than trying to tighten fasteners. If there are bronze end bushings, check for movement not greater than the specified maximum (for example, 1/8-in.) as jacking occurs. If there is excessive wear, replace the bushings.

Rubber beam center bushings should be inspected periodically for excessive wear. Normal wear is evidenced by rubber shredding from each end of the bushings. Wear is excessive when lateral movement of the axles on turns exceeds manufacturer's specifications. If the inside walls of the tires contact the suspension frame hangers, replace the bushings.

Removal

Completely drain the air brake and air suspension system (if equipped) and disconnect the air lines. Disconnect the shock absorbers and air springs (if equipped) at the lower end.

Using a suitable floor jack, raise and safely support the axle at the equalizer beam. Remove the tire and wheel assembly and remove the beam saddle caps. Remove the adapters at the axle brackets using a suitable tool, as sometimes the end caps are seized. Carefully lower the beam away from the spring saddle and slide the beam off of the beam support tube.

CAUTION: Equalizer beams are very heavy. Use care when removing the beam as it may drop to the floor.

Rebushing

Using a suitable press, remove the bushings from the beam assembly. Hone out the bushing bores with a suitable honing tool until the bushing bores are smooth. Lubricate the bushing jackets with a suitable lubricant to ease installation. Using the press, carefully install the beam bushings.

NOTE: Make sure that the beam bores are clean and the bushings are well lubricated before installation.

Inspect the beam support tube, saddles, saddle caps, spring pins and bushings while the assembly is apart and replace parts as necessary.

Installation

Slide the beam onto the beam support tube. Carefully raise the beam into the axle brackets and install the adapters. Align the beam with the spring saddle and install the saddle caps into the bottom of

Suspension System Diagnosis And Repair

the saddle. Torque all fasteners to manufacturer's specifications.

Install the tire and wheel assembly, and reconnect the shock absorbers and air springs (if equipped) at the lower end. Reconnect the air brake and air suspension system (if equipped) air lines. Torque all fasteners to manufacturer's specifications.

AIR SUSPENSIONS

The air suspension system utilizes air under pressure, which is supplied by the vehicle's air brake system. The supply comes from the portion of the system that is upstream of the treadle valve and is thus constantly pressurized.

Air is supplied to the air springs when height is too low, and is exhausted from the system when height is excessive. Ride height for the system must be maintained within plus or minus 1/4-in. for the best ride, cornering stability, and longest system component life.

Air suspensions have several major advantages. The primary one is that air pressure varies with load, maintaining ride height. Because air pressure drops as vehicle gross weight drops, a smooth ride is maintained even when the cargo box or trailer is empty. It's particularly desirable when the vehicle may need to run empty at least some of the time (for example, in petroleum products hauling).

A second advantage of air suspensions is that because rubber (a very flexible material) and air do the flexing, and because they do not endure side-to-side and fore-and-aft stresses, air springs last a long time, given the absence of road damage. Because of the fact that the articulating parts do not support the system and therefore do not need to flex, the system can be designed to give unusually high roll stiffness, which is resistance to leaning in turns.

Inspect the suspension bushings very carefully. They are replacement items that usually don't last as long as many other suspension components. When they become elongated, alignment of the axles becomes incorrect.

A quick way to see if a truck's air suspension system has developed a lot of wear in certain critical areas is to have a helper drive the vehicle down a rough road while the technician observes from the front and rear. If the vehicle's motions are straight vertical ones, with little side-to-side play, the suspension is probably in fairly good condition.

However, since minor wear may be hard to spot in this way, a very careful visual inspection should also be performed. A good guideline is to simply replace bushings every 50,000 to 100,000 miles, depending on the severity of the road surface for the application.

Shock absorbers convert the energy stored up in the air springs to heat. They also protect the springs from severe overload. Under some road conditions, the absence of the absorbing action can even trick the height control valve into over-inflating the air springs, causing an even rougher ride.

Road test the vehicle and test the shock absorbers as previously outlined. The shock absorber can also be disconnected and compressed to check its operation. Look for hydraulic leaks, which most often occur around the piston rods. Inspect shock brackets for cracks or breaks that may cause good shocks

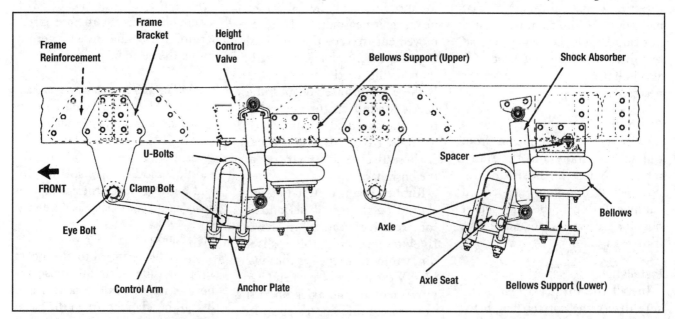

Tandem axles with air suspension are used to provide adjustable carrying heights and soft rides for delicate cargo. Air bellows may be filled with air from the main air tank.

Suspension System Diagnosis And Repair

to become ineffective. Make repairs as necessary.

Diagnosis

When all air springs are deflated, look for:
- Insufficient air in vehicle air brake system
- Leakage in the line linking the vehicle air brake system and suspension system
- Leakage in system air lines or fittings
- Defective pressure protection (check) valve (single height control valve system)
- Defective, dirty, maladjusted height control valve (single height control valve system)
- Bent, broken or disconnected height control valve linkage (single height control valve system).

When air springs are flat on one side of the vehicle only, look for:
- Leakage between height control valve and air springs (dual height control valve system)
- One or more springs on one side leaking air (dual height control valve system)
- Defective pressure protection (check) valve (dual height control valve system)
- Defective, dirty, maladjusted height control valve (dual height control valve system)
- Bent, broken or disconnected height control valve linkage (dual height control valve system)
- Inoperative height control valve (dual height control valve system).

When air springs deflate rapidly when the vehicle is parked, look for:
- Air leakage from the suspension system
- Defective pressure protection (check) valve in combination with leakage in the brake system.

If the vehicle ride height is too high or too low, look for:
- Height control valve out of adjustment
- Height control valve dirty or with slightly worn parts
- Broken shock or suspension travel stop (ride height consistently too high).

Height Control Valve

The height control valve is designed so that it actually detects the height of the frame above the axles, air spring height and degree of inflation. It is mounted on the frame, and is operated through a lever-type linkage that's connected through a vertical linkage rod and two hinges to an anchor point on an axle.

When a truck is being loaded, the weight of cargo in the trailer gradually compresses the air springs a few inches. When the truck chassis drops, the valve will drop also. This causes actuation of the valve linkage, opening the valve, and allowing air to flow into the air springs. The increased pressure soon raises the height of the frame. This change in height rotates the lever arm back to the level position, cutting off the air.

When a truck is being unloaded, the pressure in the air springs raises the height of the frame. This lowers the axle in relation to the height of the valve, causing the lever to open the valve exhaust port. As air is exhausted, the air bags deflate slightly, the frame drops, and the linkage rotates the lever arm back to the level position. In this position, the exhaust port of the height control valve is closed off.

Note that use of an effective, well-designed height control valve, kept in good operating condition, will prolong the life of all components of an air suspension system. When ride height is correct, the components operate with the stresses acting on them in ways for which they were designed. That is, with the maximum amount of energy being dampened out of the system and with a minimum of shock or overload.

If ride height is sometimes excessive as the truck rolls down the road, but levels off to an appropriate height when the truck sits, the problem could be a broken shock mount or broken suspension travel stop.

With the vehicle unloaded and on a level surface, make sure the air in the system is in excess of 80 psi throughout the procedure. Block the wheels to prevent vehicle movement. Exhaust the air from the springs, and reinflate. Then measure the distance from the ground to the center of the axle spindle on the axle nearest to the height control valve. Measure from the ground to the bottom of the frame at a point near the axle. The ride height is the difference between the two measurements.

If the air system air bags are all flat, first check the dashboard gauge to make sure there is at least 65 psi of pressure in the air brake system. Then, check the height control valve linkage to make sure it is still properly connected and that none of the parts are bent or broken. Make a careful, visual inspection of all the system parts—air lines, fittings and air springs—for damage and leaks.

Also, check to see whether or not the height control valve is leaking air with the actuating lever in the neutral (level) position. If you're unsure, check the valve by disconnecting the linkage at the dampener grommet at the axle anchor.

Move the lever up to see whether or not air flows into the air springs (hold it long enough to allow

Training for Certification

Suspension System Diagnosis And Repair

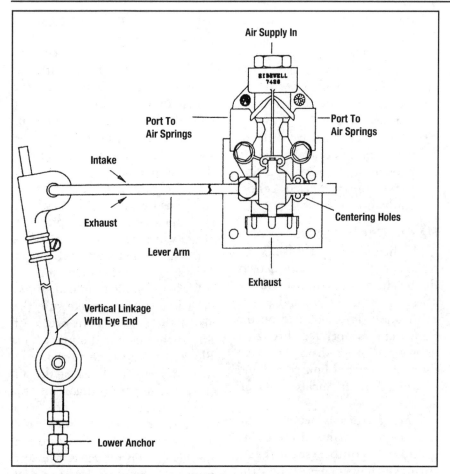

This control valve is designed to admit air to the springs of an air suspension system. The valve is mounted on the frame. The lower anchor is attached to one of the axles. The linkage thus allows the valve to adjust the height of the frame above the axles by admitting air to the air springs or exhausting air from the system. *(Courtesy: Ridewell Corp.)*

response-about 10 seconds). If it does, return the actuating arm to the neutral position. Air flow should stop. Then, lower the actuating lever to exhaust air from the exhaust port. If air is exhausted, return the lever to the neutral position. Air flow should stop.

If the valve passes these tests and there are no serious leaks in the system, a vehicle ride height problem can be corrected by adjusting the valve as specified by the manufacturer. If the valve does not allow air to pass into the system or does not exhaust air, replace or rebuild it.

Removal

Park the truck on a level surface and block the wheels to prevent vehicle movement. Completely drain the air pressure from the system. Remove the air lines to the valve. Remove the valve link from the valve assembly. Remove the locknuts, washers and bolts that connect the valve to the frame and remove the valve.

Installation

Install the valve to the frame with the attaching bolts, washers and locknuts. Torque to manufacturer's specifications. Reconnect the air lines and install the valve link. Charge the air system and check for leaks. At this time the valve can be adjusted.

Adjustment

NOTE: It is recommended that a copy of the proper vehicle ride height be kept with the truck for technical reference.

According to the Technology and Maintenance Council (TMC) of the American Trucking Associations (ATA), the following procedure should be followed when adjusting ride height:

1. With the vehicle unloaded and on a level surface, block the wheels to prevent vehicle movement. The air in the system must be in excess of 80 psi throughout the procedure.

2. Make sure the vehicle tires are properly inflated. Release the brakes. Disconnect the linkage from the valve and exhaust all the air from the air springs by rotating the control arm past the neutral position to the down position.

NOTE: Some height control valves feature a time delay feature, so allow time for valve actuation.

3. Rotate the control arm to the up position until air flows back into the air springs. Rotate the control arm to the neutral position when the ride height is according to specification.

4. According to the TMC, adjustments may involve multiple holes in brackets, jam nuts, slotted holes or even replacing the rod. If ride height needs to be adjusted by replacement of the rod, consult the manufacturer.

5. After the adjustment, recheck by disconnecting the link and deflating the air springs about half way. Reconnect the link, which will inflate the air springs. Check the ride height against specifications.

Finally, make sure all connections are retightened to manufacturer's torque specifications.

Suspension System Diagnosis And Repair

Air Springs

A routine inspection of the system will help prevent future problems. Inspect carefully for irregular wear of the springs. This is often due to misrouted air lines or dirt accumulating around the spring piston at the bottom. Accumulated dirt builds up and interferes with free operation of the spring, often causing abrasion of the outer surface and severe wear.

Reroute air lines well away from the air springs. Carefully remove accumulated dirt using only an approved solvent. These would include only non-petroleum solvents, non-organic solutions like soap and water or alcohol. Pressurized steam should not be used because it can force liquid into nooks and crannies, creating a potential for rust. Check the torque of all nuts/bolts attaching the air springs and bring them up to manufacturer's specifications.

Do not mix different brands of air springs, as they inevitably have different spring rates. Spring rate is the rate at which a spring supporting force increases as it is compressed. Naturally, using springs with different rates will cause uneven and unanticipated stresses on the suspension system.

Removal

Block the wheels to prevent vehicle movement, and completely depressurize the air system. Raise and safely support the vehicle at the frame, relieving the load from the suspension.

Remove the securing nuts and washers that connect the air spring to the mounting bracket. Remove the air spring air line, and remove the brass fittings from the spring. Remove the fasteners and washers that connect the air spring to the frame hanger, and remove the spring.

Inspect the air line, frame hanger and mounting bracket for damage. The brass air line fitting should be replaced.

Installation

Install the replacement air spring assembly onto the frame hanger and the mounting bracket. Install the fasteners and washers that connect the air spring to the mounting bracket and hanger, and torque to manufacturer's specifications.

Connect the brass air line fitting to the air spring, using a suitable sealing tape on the threads. Reconnect the air line. Lower the vehicle and charge the air system. Check for leaks and proper spring operation.

Lift Axle

Lift axles (also called tag axles) allow a truck to handle increased loads by using an additional non-powered axle either in front or behind the drive axle(s). Lift axles can be utilized on trucks, trailers, or both depending on the need. This additional axle is normally raised off the ground when not in use.

When the driver activates the lift axle cab switch, air is supplied to the lift axle air bags (called load air bags) through an air pressure regulator. The air bags inflate, pushing the lift axle to the ground. The lift axle wheels then support additional vehicle weight. When the vehicle is empty or when additional load capacity is not needed, air is exhausted from the load air bags, and depending on the application, either a steel spring, or supplemental air bags (called lift air bags) raise the axle off the ground.

Inspect the manual control operation of the lift axle by operating the in-cab switch. Ensure that the lift axle air bags inflate to the manufacturer's recommended pressure, allowing the axle to lower to the ground.

Inspect the 'loaded' suspension ride height using the manufacturer's measuring points and specifications. Because the lift axle is dependent on supply air, a minimum manufacturer's recommended air pressure must be achieved and maintained. Check the air bags, fittings, and air lines for leakage. Inspect all mounting and pivot bushings for excessive wear.

Check the shock absorbers and brackets for damage and replace as necessary. Inspect the lift axle tires for scrubbing and excessive wear. Check the wheel ends and make sure they are properly lubricated with the appropriate grease/oil. While the lift axle is essentially only a load-bearing axle, it is still equipped with brakes, so inspect the brake shoes for wear. Replace or repair components as necessary.

Some lift axles are self-steering, which allows for greater truck maneuverability for longer periods when the lift axle is supporting additional weight.

If the lift axle is not tracking properly, as witnessed by excessive lift axle tire wear, check the caster angles. Inspect all mounting bushings and steering stabilizers. If the vehicle is equipped with a self-steering axle, inspect the steering components for looseness and replace as necessary using the manufacturer's procedures.

Pinion Angle

The loading and unloading of a suspension system not only affects suspension components, but driveline components as well. As the suspension system fluctuates, driveline angles change. These driveline angles must be within tolerable limits in order for the driveshaft to properly transfer the engine's power from the transmission to the rear drive axle(s).

To measure the pinion angle in relation to the driveline, place a

Training for Certification

Suspension System Diagnosis And Repair

protractor on the top surface of the driveshaft and measure the downward angle. Next place the protract at the pinion and measure the angle of the pinion at the differential assembly. Subtract the driveshaft angle from the pinion angle and compare with manufacturer's specifications.

Excessive angles must be corrected by repair of worn suspension components, engine or transmission mounts, or replacement/adjustment of torque rods. Often a correction to the vertical alignment of a suspension component will correct excessive driveline angles.

Frame Service And Repair

All trucks have ladder-type frames, which gets its name from the resemblance to a large ladder. The principal features are two lengthwise beams supported by at least four crossmembers.

When inspecting the frame, look for:
- Cracked, loose, sagging, or broken frame side rails that would permit the truck body or cab to shift, other conditions indicating imminent collapse of frame
- Cracked, loose, or broken crossmembers that would adversely affect the support of the steering gear, fifth wheel, engine, transmission, and suspension and body parts or other major components
- 1-1/2 in. or longer cracks in the frame side rail or side rail web that is directed toward the bottom flange around the radius of the rail
- Cracks in the bottom flange of the side rail web around the radius and into bottom flange
- 1 inch or longer crack in bottom flange of side rail.

Check to see that all bolts securing the body to the frame are correct for the application, in place, and torqued to specification.

A qualified technician can remove crossmembers and spring hangers that are riveted to the frame assembly by the manufacturer. After properly disconnecting and supporting the attaching component(s), use a suitable tool to cut the rivets heads. Use caution not to cut into the frame itself. Once the rivet heads are removed, drive the rivet shafts through the frame assembly. Replacement components can be installed with bolts and nuts specifically made for the application.

Frame straightening, welding, lengthening, cutting and repairing must be performed in strict accordance with the manufacturer's recommendations. Body installations and special equipment require special techniques reserved for frame specialists. Bending, welding, cutting, or drilling holes in frame components without specialized training can adversely affect the integrity of the metal in the frame.

FIFTH WHEELS

Inspection

When inspecting the fifth wheel, look for:
- Cracks in fifth wheel plate or repair weld, or cracks extending through 20 percent or more of original weld or parent metal. Approach ramps or casting-shrinkage cracks in ribs of the body of a cast fifth wheel are permissible
- Broken, missing or deformed locking parts that prevent kingpin from being held securely
- Horizontal movement between upper and lower fifth wheel halves exceeding 1/2-in.
- If upper coupler is secured by 1/2-in. bolts, there must be at least seven bolts on each side
- For an upper coupler secured by 5/8-in. or larger bolts, there must be at least five bolts on each side

Service And Maintenance

Steam clean the unit, and then inspect the brackets and mounting hardware for:
- Cracks in the fifth wheel assembly, mounting brackets and other mounting parts
- Wear or damage to the moving parts
- Free operation of the safety lock latch spring
- Loose nuts and bolts in the unit itself or anywhere in the mounting hardware
- A securely fastened spring that shows no sign of deformation
- Proper adjustment of the locking wedge. This adjustment takes slack out of the fifth wheel. Stationary jaw and kingpin wear result if slack is incorrect.

With a trailer connected, have an assistant start the vehicle and gently rock it back and forth. As this is performed, look for excessive fifth wheel component movement.

If necessary, adjust the locking wedge as follows:
- Close the fifth wheel by tripping the release latch at the bottom of the throat using a 2-in. diameter shaft or old trailer kingpin
- Push on the wedge stop rod (the bolt head that sticks out of the side of the top plate) while measuring the motion. Push the rod in until it touches the wedge. The movement should not exceed manufacturer's specifications
- To adjust, turn the head of the stop rod until the 3/8-in. clearance is obtained.

Removal

The fifth wheel plate assembly is removed by compressing it with a suitable clamping device (this can also be done with a light trailer) to relieve the load on the bracket pins. Remove the bracket pins on both sides of the frame. Remove the clamping device and, using a hoist, lift the fifth wheel away from

Suspension System Diagnosis And Repair

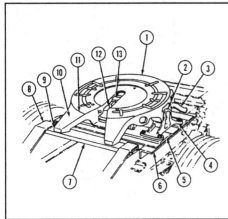

Parts of a fifth wheel:
1. Slide plate or top plate
2. Base plate pivot
3. Operating handle
4. Base plate mounting bracket
5. Mounting plate
6. Frame mounting supports
7. Skid ramp stop
8. Pick-up ramp
9. Skid ramp tips
10. Skid ramp
11. End of skid ramp
12. Throat
13. Coupler jaws

Typical fifth wheel setup. *(Courtesy: Mack Trucks Inc.)*

the frame assembly. Turn the fifth wheel over, exposing the bottom, and lower the fifth wheel onto a suitable working surface. Remove the sliding plate and mounting angles from the frame.

NOTE: If possible, do not remove the hoist from the fifth wheel, as it will be needed to lift the fifth wheel upon disassembly.

Disassembly

Fifth wheels may wear out due to lack of frequent and proper adjustment of the locking wedge. Another cause of wear is running a good fifth wheel with a worn trailer kingpin.

Even if there is little wear on the wedge stop rod and the kingpin, excessive play in the locking wedge indicates that the fifth wheel should be overhauled.

Overhaul typically involves replacing the wedge and movable jaw, together with the springs. These parts are included in an overhaul kit.

Using a hammer and a drift, drive out the fifth wheel bracket shoes on both sides. Remove the bracket pad from the casting with a suitable prying tool. Remove the spring pin from the lock assembly operating rod and disengage the rod.

WARNING: The lock spring is under compression. Remove the lock cover plate carefully.

Slide the cover plate until it clears the tabs and lift the plate from the housing. Remove the lock lever bar and the lock assembly parts. Remove the locking pins for the lock jaw assembly, and using a wood dowel, tap on the lock jaw pins to dislodge. Remove the yoke assembly. Using the hoist, carefully lift the fifth wheel and remove the lock jaws from underneath.

Assembly

Install the sliding plate and mounting angles onto the truck frame. With the fifth wheel still safely elevated, install the lock jaws from underneath. Install the yoke and insert the jaw pins through the alignment holes of the fifth wheel, and install the locking pins.

Carefully lower the fifth wheel and install the lock lever bar and lock assembly parts. Compress the lock spring with the lock cover plate while sliding the plate underneath the tabs. Install the operating rod and spring pin, and install the bracket pad into the fifth wheel casting. Install the fifth wheel bracket shoes. Using a hoist, raise the fifth wheel into position on the tractor, and install the bracket pins on both sides.

Lube the unit as follows:

• Rock the rear of the fifth wheel upward and lubricate the grease fittings on both sides until grease flows back through the fittings. Make sure grease can be seen at both the front and rear of the pivot bearing. Move the fifth wheel to the rear position, allowing grease to spread thoroughly over the bearing surface

• Close the wheel as described in the first step of the procedure for adjusting the locking wedge. Lubricate the top and bottom of the jaw and wedge. Pry the jaw and wedge apart and fill the space between them with grease

• If the fifth wheel has a slider,

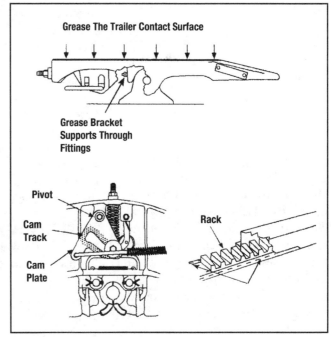

Fifth wheel lubrication points. *(Courtesy: Holland Corp.)*

Training for Certification

39

Suspension System Diagnosis And Repair

oil the locking members and other moving parts. Operate them to check for free operation.

Fifth Wheel Stops

Fifth wheel stops keep the fifth wheel from sliding from the mounting bracket assembly. These stops are welded to the fifth wheel mounting bracket at all four corners. Care must be taken when inspecting the stops to ensure that the welds are intact and that the stops themselves are not damaged or cracked.

Air Controls

Some tractors are equipped with an air control to unlock the fifth wheel. This control allows the driver to unlock the fifth wheel from the cab, using a dash-mounted valve. The system is designed to only unlock the fifth wheel if the parking brake is engaged, eliminating the possibility of accidental trailer release when the combination is in motion.

WARNING: Always follow the manufacturer's recommendations when installing or repairing pneumatic fifth wheel systems. If the manufacturer's recommendations are not followed, and the system is not properly installed or repaired, inadvertent activation of the system while the tractor-trailer is in motion could release the trailer and cause a serious accident.

When the parking brake is engaged, a diverter valve opens and allows air to flow to the dash valve. When the dash valve is actuated, air flows to the control valve at the lock cylinder, which releases the locking jaw of the fifth wheel. In case of a system malfunction, the fifth wheel can also be operated manually. The system consists of the dash control valve, a diverter valve, air lines and an air cylinder

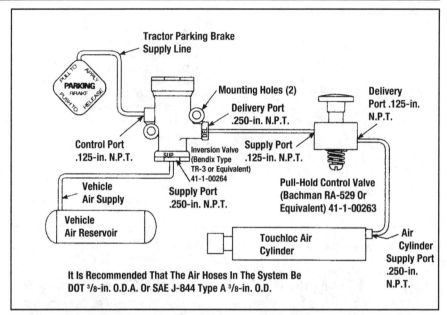

Fifth wheel air control system. *(Courtesy: ConMet Corp.)*

mechanism.

NOTE: It is recommended that the technician have a basic knowledge of air brake systems and their operation to perform repairs to fifth wheel air controls.

To check for leaks, apply the parking brake and engage the system. Coat all fittings with soapy water. There should be no leaks detected. If leaks are found, depressurize the air system and replace any leaking or malfunctioning parts as necessary.

Visually inspect the air lines and hoses for wear, chafed or badly routed lines along with other obvious damage. Also, improper routing, clamping and crimping are cause for replacement. Use the correct ferrules, inserts, and nuts when replacing an air line or hose.

PINTLE HOOKS

A pintle hook is a coupling device used in double trailer, triple trailer and truck-trailer combinations. It has a curved, fixed towing horn with an upper latch that opens to accept the drawbar eye of a trailer dolly. The drawbar is attached to the trailer. It is important to mount the pintle hook to a part of the frame with sufficient strength to support the rated capacity of the hook.

When inspecting the pintle hook, look for:

• The assembly must not be welded in an attempt to repair
• It must not have a missing or ineffective fastener
• Loose mounting or insecure latch
• Crack in the assembly or frame crossmember used for attachment
• Section reduction when coupled
• No part of horn should have width reduced by more than 20% wear.

Clean and check the pintle hook for proper operation, worn, damaged or missing parts. Replace as required. Inspect the coupling contact area and periodically disassemble the hook to inspect for wear on the shank mounting flanges. Replace any component when wear exceeds manufacturer's specifications. Regularly lubricate the latch pivot with suitable lubricant. Check the mounting fasteners for proper torque.

DRAWBAR

The drawbar is designed to fit into the pintle hook, and is used to pull double trailer, triple trailer and truck-trailer combinations. It is important to use a mounting structure on the trailer of sufficient strength to support the rated capacity of the drawbar. Also, the mounting surface must have an adequate chamfer to clear the drawbar shank fillet so that the drawbar is flush with its mounting surface.

The drawbar is mounted by removing the cotter pin, nut and washer from the drawbar, and inserting the drawbar into the mounting structure. Install the washer and nut and torque to manufacturer's specifications.

Notes

Wheel Alignment Diagnosis, Adjustment And Repair

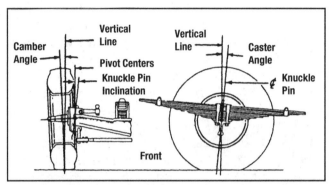

Alignment angles of camber, caster and kingpin inclination play an important part in proper vehicle handling.

Wheel alignment has become more important than ever. Alignment affects tire wear and the friction generated as the truck rolls down the road and, therefore, fuel mileage.

Suspension and steering alignment problems depend on many variables other than the parts that are obviously involved. Inspect all of the following items before attempting to correct a misalignment problem through simple adjustment alone, especially if the misalignment is severe and of a type not typical of normal wear:

- Take the vehicle on a thorough road test, looking for symptoms such as pulling to one side, wander or drift, darting, shimmy or hard steering
- Inspect front tires, rims and wheels for equal size and type, wear and correct inflation pressure
- Inspect the rear tires for proper (identical) size, type and inflation
- Check wheel bearings for excessive play
- Check for broken or sagging springs, loose spring clips or other loose parts including axle clamping plates. Torque spring clip attaching nuts. Check for wear of spring center bolts (excessive looseness)
- Check for excessive side clearance at the spring shackles. Make sure spring pins and bushings do not have excessive clearance
- Make sure the frame is properly aligned
- Make sure the steering linkage parts such as cross tubes, drag links and steering arms are free of bends and dents, and that all ball sockets are tight (not excessively worn).

Kingpin bushings and their vertical thrust bearings are also critical parts that affect all three main alignment specifications. These parts are subject to tremendous stress and wear because of the great weight carried and constant rotation from steering. They are perhaps the most critical parts to be checked for wear and repaired prior to making final alignment settings.

Attempting to simply align a front end to compensate for excessive wear or damage is bad practice and will tend to result in tire wear and vehicle handling problems. Even worse is an attempt to compensate for damage or extreme wear by using non-approved settings.

CAMBER ANGLE

Camber is the amount of front wheel inclination either toward or away from a vertical line at the vehicle center, when facing the vehicle front. Camber is spoken of and measured in degrees from the true perpendicular. If the wheel is tilted outward at the top, it has positive camber; if inward at the top, it has negative camber.

Trucks typically run a slight, positive camber with the vehicle off the front wheels. The purpose of the positive camber angle is to compensate for the normal deflection of the axle and front suspension joints as the front suspension is loaded. Thus, by preloading suspension joints and deflecting the front axle, it provides for flat tire contact with the road. Camber may also be utilized to apportion vehicle sprung weight on the spindle bearings.

Camber is not adjustable on most trucks. However, minor bending of a solid beam axle can correct some camber alignment problems if the bends are made by qualified personnel, although these adjustments are not recommended by most vehicle manufacturers, and in most cases will void the vehicle warranty. The bends may deflect the axle up to approximately 1/2-in. and should be done cold using special equipment. Do not apply heat to the axle in order to bend it as heat weakens the integrity of metal components.

INCLUDED ANGLE

Included angle is the name given to that angle which includes both inclination and camber. It is the relationship between the centerline of the wheel and the centerline of the kingpin (or the knuckle support pivots). This angle is built into the knuckle (spindle) forging and will remain constant throughout the life of the truck, unless the spindle itself is damaged.

When checking a vehicle using alignment equipment, always measure inclination as well as camber. Add the inclination to the camber for each side of the truck. These totals should be exactly the same for both sides, regardless of how far from the norm the individual readings may be.

For example, the left side of a truck checks 5 1/2 degrees inclination and 1 degree positive camber—total 6 1/2 degrees, while the right side checks 5 1/4 degrees of inclination and 1 1/4 degrees positive camber (the total, again, is 6 1/2 degrees). Since both sides check exactly the same for the included angle, it is unlikely that either spindle, in this instance, is bent (both spindles would have to have been bent identically).

Adjusting to correct for camber will automatically set correct inclination. Since camber is non-adjustable on most trucks, in most cases of an axle that has not been abused, normal inclination will be practically identical on both sides.

A bent spindle would show up like this: the left side of a truck has 3/4 degree positive camber, 5 1/4 degrees inclination — total 6 degrees included angle. The right side has 1 1/4 degrees positive camber, 6 degrees inclination — total 7 1/4 degrees included angle. Suspect a bent spindle, and if adjustments are made to correct camber, the inclination will still be incorrect due to the bent spindle. Under some conditions, making such a correction could actually make the incorrect inclination worse than before.

Since the most common cause of a bent spindle is striking the curb when parking, the side having the greater included angle usually has the bent spindle. It will be impossible to achieve good alignment and minimum tire wear unless the bent spindle is replaced.

CASTER ANGLE

Caster is the amount the kingpin is tilted towards the front or back of the vehicle when viewed from the side. Caster is usually spoken of and measured in degrees. Positive caster means that the top of the kingpin is tilted toward the back of the truck. With positive caster, the point where the kingpin axis would intersect with the road is placed ahead of the tire contact point.

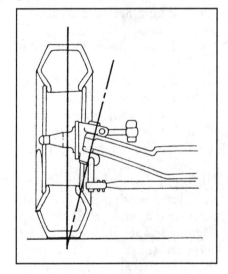

Here's how the kingpin is inclined on a typical front suspension. Note that mounting the kingpin at this angle tends to make the wheel behave much as it would if the kingpin were centered inside the wheel. That is, it removes the lever arm that would exist between the centerline of the wheel and the kingpin if the kingpin was mounted perfectly vertical.
(Courtesy: Mack Trucks, Inc.)

Negative caster is exactly the opposite, with the top of the kingpin tilted toward the front of the truck. Negative caster is sometimes referred to as reverse caster.

The effect of positive caster is to cause the truck's front wheels to return to the straight-ahead position when the steering wheel is released. This helps make it easier for the driver to keep the truck headed straight down the road and slightly counteracts the tendency for bumps to steer the truck away from a straight-ahead path.

Negative caster tends to provide easier steering effort and less directional stability. For this reason, a number of late-model trucks are designed to operate with negative caster so that the truck easily tends to steer straight on a crowned road or when driving in a crosswind.

Caster Angle Correction

Caster angle specifications are based on the vehicle load limits, which will usually result in a level frame. Since load requirements may vary, the frame does not always remain level. This fact must be considered when determining the correct caster angle. Caster increases as the chassis is loaded.

To measure the frame angle, the vehicle should be on a smooth and level surface. Place a bubble protractor on the frame rail and measure the degree of frame tilt and in what direction, either front or rear. Frame angle or tilt in excess of one degree when the vehicle is loaded to specification will cause equalizing beams on some suspensions to ride in a cocked position (so they are not parallel to the frame). This will then reduce the amount of equalizing beam rotation that is available in one direction.

If the frame angle is not level, the ride height at the tandem or front axle should be corrected. Note that if spacer plates are to be installed to raise the frame at the rear tandem, plates of equal thickness must be installed between all four spring seats and springs.

Wheel Alignment Diagnosis, Adjustment And Repair

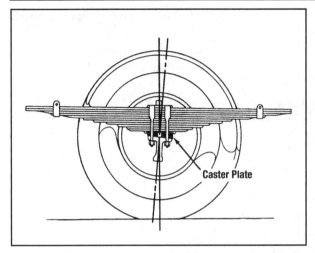

On this example, caster is adjusted by installing an appropriately tapered plate between the springs and the axle, so the axle will support the truck while sitting at an angle. *(Courtesy: Mack Trucks, Inc.)*

Two methods of determining caster angles are used. The first method is to determine the caster angle from the wheel with alignment equipment, and the second method is to obtain the desired caster angle from the kingpin tilt as measured with a protractor tool.

Always check the manufacturer's specification charts. The frame angle is then added to or subtracted from the caster angles as necessary to compensate for deviations in normal load carrying height.

It's also important to note that caster should be reasonably even on both sides of the vehicle. Always check manufacturers' specifications. Also, as in many suspension problems, incorrect caster may not simply be due to an incorrect adjustment or normal wear. Spring sag on one side will throw it off. The same thing will happen with an axle that is twisted between the knuckles and spring seats due to a severe impact or, possibly, some sort of severe overload.

On trucks with beam axles, caster is adjusted by loosening the spring U-bolt and removing or installing tapered shims between the spring and axle assembly. The taper on the shims is designed to tilt the axle assembly to the positive or negative caster angle that is desired. After the adjustment is made, torque the U-bolts to manufacturer's specifications and recheck the alignment angles.

When the vehicle pulls to one side, look for:
- Incorrect tire pressure or tire sizes not uniform
- Wheel bearings improperly adjusted
- Dragging brakes
- Improper alignment
- Grease, dirt, oil or brake fluid on brake linings
- Broken or aging springs
- Broken center or shackle bolts
- Bent front axle, linkage or steering knuckle
- Unequal shock absorber control
- Bent frame causing improper tracking
- Worn or tight kingpin bushings.

KINGPIN/STEERING AXIS INCLINATION

In addition to the caster angle, the kingpins (knuckle support pivots) are also inclined toward each other at the top. This angle is known as kingpin inclination or steering axis inclination, and is usually spoken of and measured in degrees.

The effect of inclination is to cause the wheels to steer in a straight line, regardless of outside forces such as crowned roads, crosswinds, etc., which may tend to make the vehicle steer at a tangent. It does this, in effect, by removing the lever arm that would exist between the centerline of the wheel and the centerline of the steering knuckle if the knuckle were vertical.

As the spindle is turned from extreme right to extreme left, it apparently rises and falls. Notice that it reaches its highest position when the wheels are in the straight-ahead position. In actual operation, the spindle cannot rise and fall because the wheel is in constant contact with the ground. Therefore, the truck itself will rise at the extreme right turn and come to its lowest point at the straight-ahead position, and again rise at an extreme left turn. The weight of the truck will tend to cause the wheels to come to the straight-ahead position, which is the lowest position of the truck itself.

Remember that kingpin or steering axis inclination will not directly affect tire wear, only steering stability. However, problems that cause incorrect steering inclination may cause improper camber, which in turn will cause tire wear problems.

TOE-IN

Toe-in is the amount that the front wheels are closer together at the front than they are at the back. This dimension is usually spoken of and measured in inches or fractions of an inch.

The wheels are toed-in, in part, because they are cambered. When a truck operates with 1/4+degrees camber on both left and right wheels, it will be found to operate with a pull towards the direction of positive toe (or toe-out) at both wheels.

This pull results from the combination of the camber angle, play in the joints of the cross-steering tube (especially if parts are worn), and the fact that the chassis is pushing the front wheels down the road against rolling friction. This results in an opposing force, which tight-

Training for Certification

Wheel Alignment Diagnosis, Adjustment And Repair

ens any normal allowable play in the suspension joints. This principle applies as well to the steering linkages.

Toe-in performs the function of preloading steering linkage joints and counteracts the wheel's tendency to pull outward at the front due to positive camber. As the required camber increases, generally so does the toe-in. Note that toe-in decreases as parts wear. That's why it requires regular inspection and will be maintained more consistently if the vehicle is lubricated regularly.

Remember: Caster and camber changes both have an effect on toe-in; therefore, toe-in must be the last thing corrected on the front end!

Adjustment

To adjust toe-in, make sure that the vehicle is on a level surface and in a straight-ahead position. Move the vehicle back-and-forth about 10 feet to ensure that the suspension components are settled. Block the rear wheels to prevent vehicle movement.

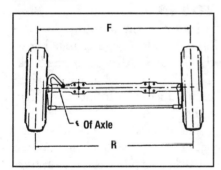

Measuring toe-in. The difference between distance F and distance R is known as toe. Most vehicles are set to toe-in when the steering wheel is in the straight-ahead position.

Raise and safely support the front of the vehicle so the front wheels are off the floor. Using a crayon or chalk, mark the center area of both front tires around the complete outer circumference of the tire (center of tread area).

Lower the vehicle and move it back-and-forth about 10 feet to ensure that the suspension components are settled.

Place a trammel bar (a long, graduated bar with two adjustable pointers located at 90 degrees to the bar) or other measuring device at the back of the tires (this can also be done with a tape measure). Align the pointers of the bar with the marks in the center of the tires. Make sure the bar is in line with the wheel hub centerline. Measure and record the distance between the two center marks on the tires.

Place the trammel bar or other measuring device at the front of the tires. Align the pointers of the bar with the marks in the center of the tires. Make sure the bar is in line with the wheel hub centerline. Measure and record the distance between the two center marks on the tires.

To obtain the toe measurement, subtract the reading at the front of the tires from the reading at the back of the tires.

Commercially available computerized alignment equipment can be used to measure and adjust toe-in. Attach the equipment using the manufacturer's instructions, and view the readings on screen. Adjust toe to the recommended specifications supplied by the alignment equipment manufacturer.

Adjust the toe by loosening the pinch bolt on each end of the tie-rod sleeve(s). Turn the sleeve until the required distance is obtained. When the measurement is obtained, torque the tie-rod pinch bolts to manufacturer's specifications and recheck the toe.

STEERING WHEEL POSITION

Always check steering wheel alignment in conjunction with, and at the same time as, toe-in. In fact, a misaligned steering wheel spoke position with the truck on a straight section of highway may

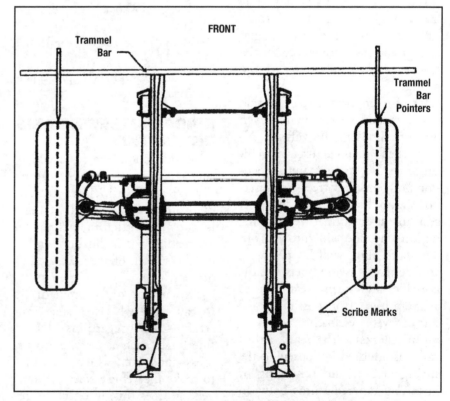

Using a trammel bar to adjust toe-in. *(Courtesy: Hendrickson Suspension)*

be the first indication of alignment problems.

If the truck has collision damage, or indicates any evidence of steering gear or linkage disturbance, the pitman arm should be disconnected from the steering linkage and turned from extreme right to extreme left positions to determine the halfway point in its turning scope. This will be the spot on the gear that is in action during straight-ahead driving and will identify which direction the steering gear should be adjusted. With the steering wheel in the straight-ahead position and the steering gear adjusted to zero lash status, reconnect the pitman arm.

When the steering wheel is not centered properly, look for:
- Steering gear set off high-spot
- Improper toe-in
- Relationship between the lengths of tie-rods is not equal
- Bent steering components
- Steering wheel improperly placed on steering shaft.

TOE-OUT STEERING RADIUS OR ACKERMAN GEOMETRY

When a truck is steered into a turn, the outside wheel of the vehicle tracks a much larger circle than the inside wheel. Therefore, the outside wheel must be steered to a somewhat less acute angle than the inside wheel. This difference in angle is often called toe-out-on-turns.

The change in angle from toe-in, in the straight-ahead position, to toe-out in the turn, is caused by the relative positions of the steering arm joints to the kingpin centerline and to each other. Because of this factor, it is essential that toe-in be checked when the wheels are in exactly the straight-ahead position.

If a line were drawn from the kingpin centerline through the center of the steering arm tie-rod attaching hole at each wheel, these lines would be found to cross almost exactly in the center of the rear axle.

Toe-out is checked using two turning plates incorporating angle scales and a pointer. Make sure toe-in is set to specifications and that the turning plate pointers indicate 0 degrees. Position vehicle so that the front wheels are on the turntables in the straight-ahead position. Turn the left front wheel to an inside turn angle of 20 degrees and read the right-side wheel angle. Note the reading. Now, repeat the process for the right wheel and note the left-side wheel angle.

A difference in outer wheel angles from side-to-side of more than a degree or so should be investigated further. If the front-end angles, including toe-in, are set correctly, and the toe-out is found to be grossly different or incorrect, suspect bent steering arm(s). A steering axis inclination measurement may help identify which side is at fault.

The steering angle and turning radius are critical to vehicle performance, both in terms of safety

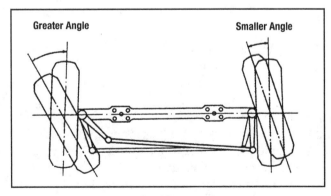

The angle formed at the steering arms and tie-rods make the wheels toe-out as they are turned off the straight-ahead position. This effect, called the Ackerman Principle, is necessary to prevent tire scrubbing as corners are turned.

and maneuverability. If the steering angle is too tight, the steering could dangerously lock up. When this angle is adjusted, and certain types of repairs have been made, the technician must adjust the front-wheel stops to provide a minimum clearance of one inch between the front tires and any chassis components.

The repairs requiring inspection of steering angle are: replacement of the front axle, replacement of a spring, front wheels aligned and any settings changed. Adjust it for both right and left hand turns, noting that, on some trucks, different limits may apply. After adjusting it, be sure to adjust the power steering gear for proper pressure relief at the new limits, if necessary.

TRACKING

While tracking is more a function of the rear axle and frame than of the front suspension, it is difficult to align the front suspension when the truck does not track straight. Proper tracking means that the centerline of the rear axle follows exactly the path of the centerline of the front axle when the truck is moving in a straight line.

On trucks that have equal tire tread—front and rear—the rear tires will follow in exactly the tread of the front tires when moving in a straight line. However, there are many trucks where the rear tread is wider than the front tread, or which use dual tires and wheels. On such trucks, the rear axle tread or dual tires will straddle the front axle tread an equal amount on both sides when moving in a straight line.

One quick way to visually check tracking is to drive directly in the back of the truck while watching it move in a straight line down a level road. Observe

Wheel Alignment Diagnosis, Adjustment And Repair

as near to the center of the truck as possible and even with the difference in perspective between the front and rear wheels, the observer can see whether or not the vehicle is tracking properly. If the truck appears to track incorrectly, the difficulty will be found in either the frame or in the alignment of the rear axle.

A more accurate method of checking tracking is to park the truck on a level floor and drop a plumb line from a point on the extreme outer edge of the front suspension. Use the same drop point on each side of the truck. Make an X chalk mark where the plumb line strikes the floor. Do the same with the rear axle, selecting a point on the rear axle housing for the plumb line.

Measure diagonally from the left rear mark to the right front mark and from the right rear mark to the left front mark. These two diagonal measurements should be exactly the same. A 1/4-in. variation is acceptable.

If the diagonal measurements taken are different, measure from the right rear mark to the right front mark and from the left rear to the left front. These two measurements should also be the same, within 1/4-in.

In addition, commercially available computerized alignment equipment can be used to measure vehicle tracking. Attach the equipment using the manufacturer's instructions, and view the readings on screen.

If the diagonal measurements are different but the longitudinal measurements are the same, the frame is swayed (diamond-shaped).

However, in the event that the diagonal measurements are unequal, the longitudinal measurements are also unequal, and the truck is tracking incorrectly, the rear axle is misaligned.

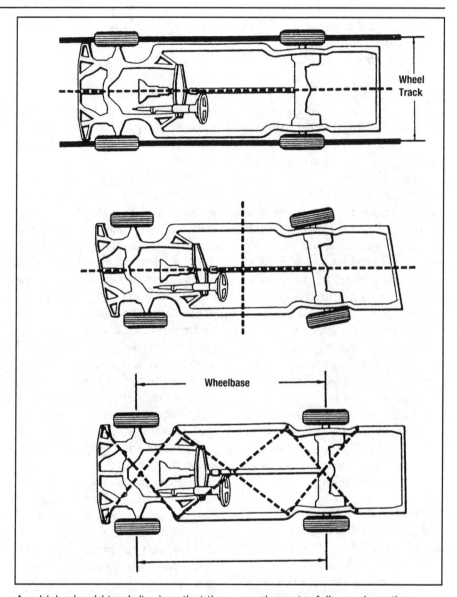

A vehicle should track (top) so that the rear axle center follows along the centerline between the vehicle's front wheels. Occasionally, a collision will disturb a frame or suspension and change tracking. Diamond frame (center) is an example of track problems. Measurement of wheelbase at X points on the frame (bottom) can diagnose a frame or suspension misalignment.

If the diagonal and longitudinal measurements are both unequal but the truck appears to track correctly on the street, a kneeback is indicated.

A kneeback means that one complete side of the front suspension is bent back. This is often caused by crimping the front wheels against the curb when parking the vehicle, then starting up without straightening the wheels out.

The steering angle and turning radius are critical to vehicle performance, both in terms of safety and maneuverability. If the steering angle is too tight, the vehicle could dangerously lock up. When this angle is adjusted, and certain types of repairs have been made, the technician must adjust the front-wheel stops to provide a minimum clearance of one inch between front tires and any chassis components.

The repairs requiring inspection

Wheel Alignment Diagnosis, Adjustment And Repair

of steering angle are: replacement of the front axle, replacement of a spring, front wheels aligned and any settings changed. Adjust it for both right and left hand turns, noting that, on some trucks, different limits may apply. After adjusting it, be sure to adjust the power steering gear for proper pressure relief at the new limits, if necessary.

REAR SUSPENSION ALIGNMENT

The rear suspension can be checked for alignment in relation to the frame and front wheels with the use of common tools, such as a carpenter's (framing) square, straightedge, plumb, length of string (cord) and/or a trammel bar. Commercially available computerized alignment equipment can also be used to measure rear suspension alignment. Attach the equipment using the manufacturer's instructions, and view the readings on screen.

Adjustment procedures vary from changing shims and adjustment of torque rod length to the turning of eccentric bolt and washer assemblies. The following are several methods of adjusting rear axle alignment:

Method A

Locate a point on both frame rails for a measuring device, such as a straightedge, to run perpendicular from the frame to the ground. The distance is optional but must be the same measurement on both sides.

Attach a long string (cord) to an object behind the rear axle. Be sure the string reaches to the measuring device or beyond. Position two 1×2×2-in. wooden blocks on the rear-wheel rim bead; one forward of the rim and the second on the rear of the rim at axle height.

Measure the distance between the string and the measuring device and record. Repeat the measuring operation on the opposite side of the axle. The two distances (left and right sides) should be equal. If not, the rear axle housing must be adjusted.

By moving the wheels 180 degrees and remeasuring, a bent wheel can be found by the difference in the measurements.

Method B

Clamp a straightedge to the top of the frame rail ahead of the forward rear axle. Use a framing square against the straightedge and the outside surface of the frame side rail to ensure the straightedge is perpendicular to the frame.

Suspend a plumb bob from the straightedge in front of the tire and on the outboard side of the forward rear axle. Next, position a bar with pointers that can be engaged in the center holes of the rear axles. Measure the distance between the cord of the plumb bob and the pointer on the forward axle and record.

Position the plumb bob and bar on the opposite side of the vehicle and measure. Record the result. Any difference in dimensions from side-to-side must be equalized if the difference exceeds 1/8-in.

Equalize the dimensions by loosening the clamp bolts on the lower adjustable torque rod for the forward rear axle and adjusting the length of the torque rod. Tighten the clamp bolts.

Before adjusting the lower torque rods, remove one end of the left and right upper torque rods on the forward rear axle to relieve any stress, which may be present due to an improperly adjusted torque rod.

Reposition the bar pointers to the axle center on each side. If any differences exist in the center-to-center measurement after the forward rear axle has been squared to the frame, the rear axle must also be aligned.

To align the rear axle, loosen the clamp bolts on the lower adjustable torque rod and adjust to equalize the center-to-center distance between the axle ends.

Method C

(For typical four-spring heavy-duty suspensions)

Position the tractor on a level floor. Slowly move the vehicle back and forth by hand (to avoid use of brakes) to free and center all suspension joints. If the suspension has them, make sure the equalizing beams are essentially level.

Block the front wheels to prevent vehicle movement and make sure all brakes are released. Position a perfectly straight piece of bar stock on the top of the frame as far forward of the drive axles as possible. Use a carpenter's square to locate the bar exactly at 90 degrees to the frame on either side. Then, secure it by clamping between the stock and the top frame flange with C-clamps.

Use a trammel bar to measure the distance from the rear edge of the straight edge to the centerline of the rear drive axle (center drilled holes in the axle shaft flanges) on

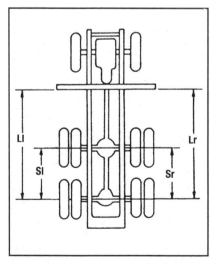

Measurements used for Method C of rear suspension alignment.
(Courtesy: Hendrickson Suspension)

Wheel Alignment Diagnosis, Adjustment And Repair

both sides (Ll on the left and Lr on the right).

If the dimensions are within 3/16-in., alignment of the rear drive axle is satisfactory. If the difference is more than 3/16-in., adjust the position of the axle as specified in the next step.

To adjust the axle, loosen the torque rod bar pin locknuts on the center spring hanger of the side with the longer dimension and add drop-in shims. These shims go directly in front of the spring hanger, on the bolt that fastens the torque rod to the forward hanger via the torque rod bar pin, on Hendrickson four spring suspensions. Note that the bar pin must always be mounted adjacent to the forward face of the spring hanger legs. Four shims totaling 1/4-in. thickness is the maximum permitted. Snug the nuts, but don't fully torque them.

Measure the distance between the centerlines of the forward drive axle and the rear drive axle (center drilled holes in the axle shaft flanges) with the trammel bar (Sl on the left and Sr on the right). Make adjustments on the forward spring hangers as in the previous step, as necessary. Snug the locknuts.

Move the vehicle back-and-forth several times and then recheck alignment to make sure the adjustments are correct. Torque the rod bar pin locknuts to 150-205 ft.-lbs. and remove the straightedge.

Notes

Wheels, Tires and Hub Diagnosis And Repair

TIRE TYPES AND CONSTRUCTION

Two types of tires are used, either tube or tubeless, and are constructed in three categories: bias-ply, belted-bias and radial-ply construction. Fiberglass or steel belts are used in the belted-bias and radial-ply construction.

Tires are designed for either on-highway or off-highway use and should never be interchanged. The tires should be of the proper size, properly inflated and in good condition. They should have no sidewall breakage or damage and must have sufficient tread.

Tires have a particular tread pattern most suitable for two basic positions: steer axle and drive axle. The goal is to provide maximum life in each position under the particular types of stresses encountered. Steer axle tires obviously need to provide a maximum of cornering force, and drive axle tires a maximum of traction under acceleration.

Rib-type tires, which have bands of tread that run continuously around the tire's circumference, provide optimum fuel economy. However, drive axle tires with small blocks or sections of tread (lugs) are preferred over rib tires when traction is important.

Basic tire designs share a common casing. When tread is worn, the casing can be retreaded with a different type tread and used in a different wheel position. It can also be used in a different geographic section of the country, where traction requirements are different or as required by the customer.

Because of the very high dollar value of a tire casing, tire maintenance is absolutely critical. This also has a critical emphasis on road safety. Not only must tires always be properly inflated and loaded only to capacity, but proper repair is critical as well.

A tire that has been penetrated by a nail or similar road debris cannot be run for a significant length of time unless it is removed from the rim and sealed at the inner liner, as well as receiving a vulcanized patch on the tread. Failure to repair a tire properly will ultimately allow moisture into the tire. This can cause rusting of the steel belts and a possible blowout or, at the very least, the inability to reuse the casing for retreading.

TIRE INSPECTION

Proper inflation is absolutely critical to tire life. Inflation pressure must be geared precisely to the load the tire carries and, ideally, reduced as load is reduced and increased as load is increased.

The operator must be particularly careful to monitor gross weight and use tires of the proper ratings so tires do not run overloaded, even by a small margin. Running fully loaded with under-inflated tires, or even running with full pressure but slightly over-

Tire construction and nomenclature. Mixing of tire construction types on a given axle is not recommended.

Wheels And Tires Diagnosis And Repair

loaded will contribute to heating and shortened life.

The reason for this is that pressurized air is actually a critical part of the tire's structure as it rolls down the road, and each section is repeatedly compressed and expanded when it contacts the pavement.

Federal Motor Carrier Safety Regulations include a chart which lists inflation pressures for tires according to the load each tire carries. Always make sure tire pressures are maintained at the correct value according to this chart.

It is also important to understand that tires must either be checked when cold, or the pressure must be adjusted for the heating effect of operation. For example, the Federal Motor Carrier Safety Regulations specify that a tire rated to carry 4,000 lbs. or more and to run at an average speed of 41 to 55 mph during the previous hour shall be inflated to 15 psi beyond the standard cold operating pressure. Tires with a rating under 4,000 lbs. should be inflated to 5 psi more than the cold inflation pressure.

Running dual wheels with one tire flat, which causes critical overheating of the tire carrying the entire load may even cause the flat tire to lose tread or even catch fire due to scrubbing the tread along the road.

While tread wears relatively rapidly and lasts only a year or two (100,000 to, at maximum, 200,000 miles), the casing itself—the tire's basic structure—is an extremely expensive, durable and reusable item.

When inspecting tires, look for:

Steer Axle
- Tube-type radial must have suitable tube stem marking, either a red band or the word radial embossed or molded on the stem
- Bias and radial tires must not be mixed on the same axle
- Tire flap must not be protruding through the valve slot in the rim and touching the stem
- Use of a re-grooved tire is prohibited
- Weight carried exceeds the limit, including the limit allowed for the specific pressure
- The tire must not contact the body or frame either because of suspension misalignment or damage or overloading
- Tires must not have a tread depth of less than the specified dimension in two adjacent tread grooves anywhere on the tire. The dimension is 2/32-in.
- Tires must not have a portion of the breaker strip or casing ply visible in the tread
- The sidewall must not be cut or damaged so as to expose the ply cord
- Must not be labeled 'not for highway use' in a highway application
- The tire must not have a bulge suggesting tread or sidewall separation. A legitimate exception is a bulge not exceeding 3/8-in. from a section repair, which is often labeled with a blue triangle
- The tire must, of course, not be flat or have a leak that can be felt or heard.

Drive Axle
- The weight carried must not exceed the tire's load limit, including the limit allowed for the pressure
- Must not be labeled 'not for highway use' in a highway application
- Tires must not have a tread depth of less than the specified dimension in two adjacent tread grooves anywhere on the tire. On drive and trailer axles, the dimension is 1/32-in.
- A section of tread missing, if the area of the loss extends to 75 percent of the tread width and more than 12 inch of tire circumference, is prohibited
- The tire must not contact the body or frame because of suspension misalignment, damage, or overloading
- The tire must not be flat or have a leak that can be felt or heard
- Bias-ply tires must not have more than one ply exposed in the tread area or sidewall; an exposed area of the top of the ply must not exceed 2 sq. inch (both dual tires must have the defect to put the vehicle out of service)
- Radial tires must not have two or more plies exposed in the tread area, damaged cords evident in the sidewall or an exposed area of cords on the sidewall that exceeds 2 sq. inch (both dual tires must have the defect to put the vehicle out of service)
- The tire must not have a bulge suggesting tread or sidewall separation. A legitimate exception is a bulge not exceeding 3/8-in. from a section repair, which is often labeled with a blue triangle
- The tire must not be mounted or inflated so that it contacts any part of the vehicle or, with dual tires, its mate.

WEAR PATTERNS

Tire wear patterns can indicate the accuracy of alignment and condition of suspension components.

For example, if a tire has too much toe-in or toe-out, the tires are not riding straight down the road. This can result in a wear pattern called feathering, where one edge of the tread will wear more than the other edge. Feathering can be felt by running the palm of your hand at a 90-degree angle across the tread surface.

When excessive camber is present (either positive or negative), tires will wear on one edge of the circumference of the tire only. In addition to sagging springs or

Wheels And Tires Diagnosis And Repair

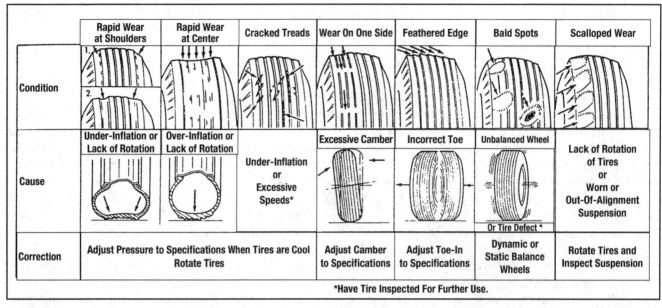

Learn to read the tread of the tires. Wear patterns can tell a tale of air pressure, steering and suspension malfunctions.

worn suspensions parts, if the tire is worn on the outside, suspect excessive positive camber. If the tire is worn on the inside, suspect excessive negative camber.

A scalloped or dished tire tread condition usually indicates the tire is bouncing excessively as it rolls down the road. This condition is usually caused by, but not limited to, improper tire balance, over-inflation, loose suspension and steering components or worn shock absorbers. Vibration, shimmy and tire tramp can all be indications of these conditions.

When experiencing uneven tire wear, look for:
- Tire pressures low
- Excessive camber
- Failure to rotate tires
- Tires out of balance
- Tires overloaded
- Unequal tire size
- Out-of-round tires and rims
- Incorrect alignment
- High speed driving into turns
- Quick starts and stops
- Uneven brake application
- Improper tracking
- Bent or worn steering and suspension components.

When the vehicle exhibits excessive vertical wheel motion (wheel tramp), look for:
- Incorrect tire pressure
- Improper balance of wheels, tires and brake drums
- Loose tie-rod ends or steering connections
- Worn or inoperative shock absorbers
- Excessive run-out of brake drums, wheels or tires.

WHEELS AND RIMS

The inspection of wheels and rims is most important to prevent abnormal steering linkage and tire wear. Bent rims, along with rims that have been operated in a loose condition and have the stud holes elongated or cracked, should not be used.

The wheels can be checked for radial (out-of-round) or lateral (wheel side wobble) runout while on the vehicle. Check for cracks, corroded areas and damaged or cracked rings. Aluminum disc wheels are used on certain vehicle applications and a reasonable amount of care must be exercised when mounting or demounting tires to avoid nicks and gouges in the sealing areas.

Disc Wheels

Hub piloted disc wheels are centered on the wheel hub by means of indents built into the hub assembly. The center hole of the disc rests on these indents and centers the wheel. Two-piece flange nuts make contact with the face of the disc at the stud hole. There is no ball seat at the stud hole, since the flange nuts tighten flat against the disc wheel.

Stud piloted disc wheels use the securing nuts to center the wheel onto the hub assembly. These wheels have a ball seat at the stud hole, and wheel centering occurs when the securing nuts are tightened in the proper fashion.

WARNING: Although they may have the same bolt hole patterns, don't mix hub piloted disc wheels and their hardware with stud piloted disc wheels. Damage to wheels or studs, and possible wheel loss, can result.

After the wheel has been removed and the tire has been dismounted, using all applicable safety precautions, make sure all the sealing surfaces are clean and

Wheels And Tires Diagnosis And Repair

free of debris. Inspect the wheel for pitting, cracks, rust or corrosion, elongated bolt holes or damage such as bent components. Inspect the valve stem and replace it along with a new grommet or seal if necessary. At the very least, replace the valve core if the stem is found to be in good condition.

A good practice is to paint steel rims using a metal primer to protect them from corrosion, giving the paint plenty of time to dry. Do not use paint on aluminum rims.

Before sealing the tire to the rim, lubricate the bead area with a suitable bead lubricant. Using all applicable safety precautions, mount the tire and inflate it using a safety cage.

Before mounting the tire/wheel assembly, check the studs, nuts, indents and hub mounting faces, making sure they are not damaged and are free from dirt, corrosion and debris. Make sure you are using the correct fasteners for the application. Remember, fasteners used in a stud piloted system cannot be used in a hub piloted system.

NOTE: *Never use lubricant on ball seats or mounting faces of wheels. However, suitable lubricant can be used sparingly on the threads of the studs and/or nuts.*

Install the front or inner dual wheel over the studs, being careful not to damage the threads. On the stud piloted system, lift the wheel to center a stud within a bolt hole and install a nut finger tight. Install the other nuts finger tight, and torque according to the manufacturer's tightening sequence and torque specifications.

On the hub piloted system, rotate the hub so that one indent is at the 12 o'clock position. Install a single wheel or inner dual wheel onto the hub, being careful not to damage the threads, making sure the wheel is fully seated against the drum.

Install the nuts finger tight at the 12 o'clock and 6 o'clock positions, then install the remaining nuts finger tight. Torque the nuts to about 50 ft-lbs using a criss-cross pattern. Then, torque to manufacturer's specifications. Retorque the wheel a short time after installation (50 to 100 miles) to ensure full seating.

Cast Spoke Wheels

The spoke wheel uses clamps to secure the tire/rim assembly to the wheel by means of hex nuts. The spoke wheel may have three, five or six spokes. Dual rims make use of a spacer band that is designed to hold the rims apart, providing proper spacing.

NOTE: *Always use the correct spacer band, rim, clamp and fasteners for the particular application.*

After the tire/rim assembly has been removed and the tire has been dismounted, using all applicable safety precautions, make sure all surfaces are clean and free of debris. Inspect for pitting, cracks, rust or corrosion, stripped studs or incorrectly matched parts. Inspect the valve stem and replace it along with a new grommet or seal if necessary. At the very least, replace the valve core if the stem is found to be in good condition. Inspect the spacer bands for damage or distortion.

A good practice is to paint steel rims using a metal primer to protect them from corrosion, giving the paint plenty of time to dry.

Before sealing the tire to the rim, lubricate the bead area with a suitable bead lubricant. Using all applicable safety precautions, mount the tire and inflate it using a safety cage.

For single wheels, align the locators between the wheel spokes and place the rim and inflated tire on the cast spoke wheel. For dual wheels, align the locators between the wheel spokes and place the inside rim over the wheel as far as possible. Install the spacer band onto the wheel using constant pressure on both sides.

NOTE: *Make sure the spacer band is installed evenly on all sides of the wheel.*

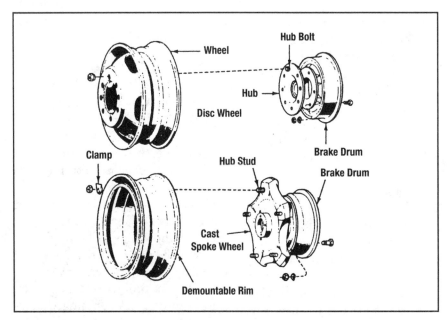

Construction comparisons of disc and cast spoke wheel assemblies. Either wheel must be torqued properly when mounted to prevent excessive runout. There are different procedures for each design.

Training for Certification

Wheels And Tires Diagnosis And Repair

Install the outer rim into position and secure the clamps evenly around the outer circumference. Snug the nuts according to manufacturer's specifications. Do not tighten the nuts fully until all of them have been snugged. This allows the rim to self-align with the cast wheel. Once the nuts have all been snugged, torque according to the manufacturer's tightening sequence and torque specifications. Retorque the wheel a short time after installation (50 to 100 miles) to ensure full seating.

When inspecting wheels, look for:
- The locking ring must not be bent, broken, cracked, improperly seated, sprung or mismatched
- The rim must not be cracked circumferentially except at the valve stem hole
- A disc wheel must not be cracked between any two holes, regardless of type of hole
- A disc wheel must not have two cracks of any kind or dimension
- A disc wheel must not have one crack that exceeds 3 inches in length
- A disc wheel must not have 50 percent or more of the stud holes elongated
- A spoke wheel must not have two or more cracks of 1 inch or greater in length across spoke or hub sections
- A spoke wheel must not have two or more web areas cracked
- A tubeless demountable adapter must not be cracked
- There must not be cracks at three or more spokes
- Fasteners of the number specified must not be loose, missing, broken, cracked or stripped. For a ten-hole wheel, there must not be three missing or defective fasteners or two adjacent missing or defective fasteners. For a wheel with eight holes or fewer, having any two fasteners missing or defective puts it out of service.

INSPECTION OF STUDS AND NUTS

Regardless of the type of wheel used on the vehicle, the studs and nuts should be inspected. Look for damage to the threads of the ends of the studs, abnormal wear on the stud shafts caused by loose nuts or studs, broken studs or studs that have stripped threads.

Check the stud nuts for cracks, abnormal wear and stripped threads. Should a single stud be broken or damaged, the entire group of studs should be replaced to avoid future failure. This possibility may not be detectable during an examination of the studs or nuts.

Torquing studs/nuts to the proper value is critical to operating safety. Also critical is retorquing a short time after installation (50 to 100 miles) to ensure full seating. Retorquing at an appropriate interval even when wheels are not removed is also an important adjunct to operating safety. Consult the manufacturer's specifications for torque values and procedures and retorquing mileage intervals.

CHECKING AND ADJUSTING RUNOUT

Runout is the up-and-down (radial) and side-to-side (lateral) movement of the tire or wheel when it is rotating. A tire or wheel that is out of round or not running true cannot only contribute to driver discomfort and increased operating costs, it can be a safety concern.

Give the vehicle a thorough road test with the driver, noting the vehicle speed and engine rpm at which the problem occurs. Look for any unusual handling characteristics, or occurrences when the transmission is in or out of gear.

If the vibration is in the steering wheel, chances are there's a problem in the front tires. If the vibration is in the seat or chassis, suspect a rear tire problem. In addition, if the vehicle hauls a trailer while the vibration occurs, and the vibration leaves when the trailer is disconnected, the failure can be attributed to the trailer tires.

Look at the tire and wheel assemblies, checking for damage, bends, excessive wear, cupping and proper inflation. Check for proper wheel weight installation, and inspect front end components such as steering linkages, springs, shocks and bushings. Repair or replace any defective or worn parts as necessary.

To check lateral runout:
- On wheels with demountable rims, make sure the rim clamp nuts are torqued to manufacturer's specifications. On disc wheels, make sure all lugs and studs are present, and torqued to manufacturer's specifications.
- When checking tire runout, position a suitable dial indicator on the sidewall of the tire at about mid-point, and slowly rotate the tire. Compare the dial indicator readings with manufacturer's specifications.
- When checking wheel runout, position the dial indicator on a flat, clean surface of the wheel assembly, and slowly rotate the tire. Compare the dial indicator readings with manufacturer's specifications.
- If lateral runout is not within specifications on cast spoke wheels, loosen and retorque the rim clamp nuts following manufacturer's procedures. If lateral runout is not within specifications on disc wheels, remove the wheel and clean the mating surfaces. Reinstall the wheel and recheck the lateral runout.

Wheels And Tires Diagnosis And Repair

To check radial runout:
- Position a suitable dial indicator on the center tread area of the tire, and slowly rotate the tire. Compare the dial indicator readings with manufacturer's specifications.
- If radial runout is not within specifications on cast spoke wheels, loosen and retorque the rim clamp nuts following manufacturer's procedures.
- If the total runout is not within specifications for disc wheels, deflate the tire using all applicable safety precautions and separate it from the rim. Lubricate the rim and rotate the tire 180 degrees on the rim. Reinflate the tire using all applicable safety precautions and recheck runout.

BALANCING

Tire and wheel balancing is the uniform distribution of weight around the wheel and tire assembly axis of rotation. Two methods are used to balance the assemblies: static (stationary) or dynamic (running) balance. While static imbalance demonstrates a hopping or 'wheel tramp' symptom, dynamic imbalance usually causes vibration that can be felt in the steering wheel.

Various machines are available for the purpose of measuring and adjusting imbalance, and the manufacturers' recommended instructions should be followed.

Static imbalance can be measured using a static tire balancer. The tire and wheel assembly is placed horizontally on the static balancer, and gravity causes the assembly to lean to the heaviest side. This is an indication of static imbalance. Weights are added to the opposite, or lightest side of the wheel assembly so the heavy side is counteracted.

Dynamic balancing entails using a machine to measure the 'running' weight distribution of a tire and wheel. Checking dynamic balance can be done with either an on-vehicle balancer or by removing the tire and wheel assembly to install it on a balancing machine. Using either method, the tire is spun to accurately record the weight distribution. If the tire is imbalanced, the machine will recommend areas on the rim to install counteracting weights.

NOTE: On-vehicle balancers cannot be used to balance drive wheels.

Dynamic balancing is the preferred method if long tire life and smooth operation are to be achieved. However, it must be repeated at regular intervals if normal changes in balance are to be corrected. Also, because of the sheer size and expense, heavy truck dynamic balancing equipment may not be available at some shops. The technician must inspect the wheel regularly for missing weights and rebalance the assembly if a weight has fallen off the wheel.

Certain types of materials are marketed for the purpose of balancing the tire by installing a fine grain or liquid material inside the tire via the valve stem. These operate according to valid scientific principles and can achieve good balance that compensates for changes in the tire as it runs over a long period of time. However, the technician must be assured that the material is inert (will not damage the inner liner of the tire) before installing it.

If the vehicle or steering exhibits excessive shimmy, look for:
- Badly worn and/or unevenly worn tires
- Wheels and tires out of balance
- Excessive wheel or tire runout
- Worn or loose steering linkage parts
- Worn kingpins and bushings
- Loose steering gear adjustments
- Loose wheel bearings
- Improper caster setting
- Weak or broken springs or shackles
- Loose U-bolts connecting axle to spring
- Incorrect tire pressure or tire sizes not uniform
- Faulty shock absorbers
- Power cylinder loose at bracket
- Power cylinder not aligned in same plane as tie-rod
- Improper valve spool nut adjustment allowing control valve end-play
- Loose steering gear mounting bolts
- Worn or out-of-round brake drum or rotor (shimmy felt upon brake application).

MATCHING

Proper tire matching is essential on any dual wheel, and especially on tandem drive units, to avoid excessive tire wear, scuffing and possible excessive wear of the drive unit. Most manufacturers recommend the tires to be matched to within 1/8-in. of the same rolling radius or 3/4-in. of the same rolling circumference. They should also be matched as closely as possible in terms of construction and tread type, and kept as close as possible to the same inflation pressure.

TIRE REPLACEMENT

To avoid personal injury, always follow the manufacturer's instructions when using specialized tools to mount and dismount tires. Inspection of the rim parts for distortion is critical; they must never be reused unless in perfect shape. Careful reassembly so parts will mesh properly is also critical to safety.

For the safety of the repairman, the acronym D.I.P. should be remembered when working with tires and wheels.

Wheels And Tires Diagnosis And Repair

D—DEFLATE the tire before working on it.

I—INSPECT the rim, rings, lug holes and tires for damage, including distortion and proper sealing.

P—PROTECT yourself by placing the tire and wheel assembly in an inflation cage before inflating.

When replacing tubeless tires on any type of rim, it is essential that only the proper equipment be used. The technician must never pound on the bead with a hammer to break it. Instead, only specialized hand tools or a quality tire machine must be used— tools that will preserve the structure of the bead. In addition, petroleum solvents that soften rubber must never be used to break the bead; use only an approved fluid.

Finally, a technician must never use explosive force to get a tire to expand and seal onto the one-piece rim. In some cases an inflation ring can be used to close the gap between the top edge of the tire and the rim, and it will expand out of the way as air pressure is released into the tire.

Before sealing the tire to the rim, lubricate the bead area with a suitable bead lubricant. Using all applicable safety precautions, mount the tire and inflate it using a safety cage.

ROTATION

The tire rotation method used is normally dependent upon the tires, the type of vehicle being operated, and the maintenance program being followed. A general practice is to break-in new tires on the front and move them rearward when a predetermined tread thickness has been worn from the tire.

It is best to retread tires as necessary, rather than running them down to minimum tread depths. On tractors, it is best to use the proper types of tires in each of the basic types of wheel positions to ensure good traction while providing good fuel economy and long tire life.

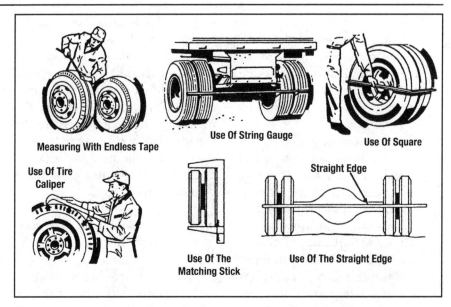

There are several methods to check comparative wheel sizes in order to match dual tires on an axle.

Rotate tires of the same type among their various wheel positions for longest life. All tires, even radials, can be rotated in either direction; the sole exception is tires with an asymmetrical tread pattern. This is a pattern that's different on the one side of the tire, and intended to be located on the side of the wheel away from the chassis at all times.

Thus, the two front-axle tires may typically be switched from side-to-side; the four tires on a single drive axle may be switched from side-to-side of the truck; and the eight tires on the tandem drive axles may be X-ed.

Such rotation will equalize wear patterns (which vary slightly on every axle and significantly on a tandem drive-axle arrangement), as well as removing the destructive effects of any form of irregular wear. Repair cuts and nicks in the tread for longest life at time of rotation.

WHEEL BEARINGS

In addition to malfunctioning suspension and steering system components, worn hubs and wheel bearings can also contribute to poor handling. Many apparent problems that persist after worn suspension and steering parts have been replaced can actually be traced back to misadjusted or worn out wheel bearings.

When the wheel bearings are inspected for looseness on any axle, be sure the brakes are fully released and the axle is safely raised off the floor. To inspect the bearings for excessive play, grasp the tire at the top and move it back and forth, or place a bar under the tire assembly and lift the bar and release it. If looseness in the bearings is present, the wheel assembly will move laterally.

There are two basic types of wheel ends, unitized and conventional. Unitized wheel ends are a complete packaged system with bearings, seals, and lubricant. Since the bearing adjustment is pre-set at the manufacturer, if there is a malfunction, the entire wheel end must be replaced.

Note the movement of the drum or rotor in relation to a stationary part of the brake backing plate or a suspension component. The average play should be within manufacturer's specifications. If applicable, adjust the bearing by first preloading the bearing to the cup and then releasing the preload. Tighten the adjusting nut to obtain the average allowed play, or the play specified by the manufacturer.

Both grease and oil-type lubrication is used with wheel bearings. Be sure of the type that is used on the vehicle before attempting to lubricate. Always replace seals when packing a bearing with grease. Replace wheel oil seals at the first sign of leakage, when lubricant needs to be added frequently, or whenever disassembly is necessary.

Two types of bearings are used for wheels, ball bearings and tapered roller bearings. Generally, tapered rollers are somewhat more forgiving and tolerant of preset torque. If a bearing is suspect, remove it and carefully inspect the working surfaces of not only the bearing, but also the spindle and hub assembly. You are looking for two flaws, abrasion damage and discoloration, such as heat bluing.

Abrasion damage can be the beginning of a crack that would allow the spindle or hub to fail catastrophically. Metal bluing indicates a change of internal crystalline structure of the metal. It has become hardened and is no longer strong enough to support the kinds of forces transmitted through a wheel/hub/spindle assembly.

Remember to discard the seal and replace it with a new one when you are removing the bearing.

Different types of adjusting nuts and locking nut assemblies are used for different applications. Do not attempt to interchange or mismatch the locking nut assemblies since locking capability can be lost.

If the vehicle has one wheel end locking nut, make sure it is preloaded using the manufacturer's specific procedures and torque settings. If a castellated nut assembly is used, install a new cotter pin. Never reuse the old one.

If the vehicle has two wheel end locking nuts, after torqueing the inner locknut to manufacturer's specifications, install the locking ring (if equipped) over the inner locknut. Next, install the outer locknut and torque to manufacturer's specifications.

Notes

Prepare yourself for ASE testing with these questions on MEDIUM/HEAVY-DUTY TRUCK SUSPENSION AND STEERING

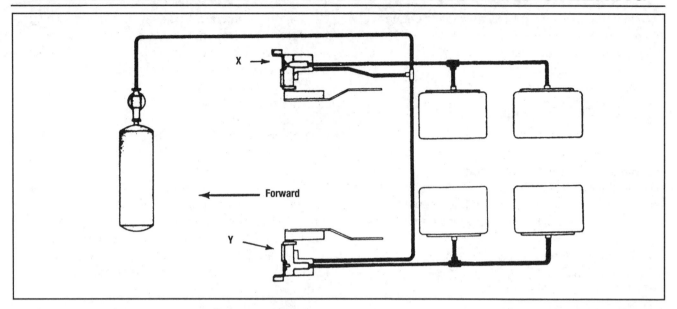

1. The truck with the air suspension system shown above leans to the right. Technician A says that valve X could be the cause. Technician B says that valve Y could be the cause. Who is right?
   A. Technician A only
   B. Technician B only
   C. Both A and B
   D. Neither A or B

2. The driver of a truck says that he hears a clattering noise from the front axle when driving on a rough road. Technician A says the cause could be worn shock absorber mounting bushings. Technician B says the cause could be worn shackle bushings. Who is right?
   A. Technician A only
   B. Technician B only
   C. Both A and B
   D. Neither A or B

3. The driver of a truck that has just had its front springs and hangers replaced says that it is hard to keep the steering wheel in a straight-ahead position. Technician A says the cause could be that the caster shims were installed backwards. Technician B says the cause could be that the wrong spring hangers were installed. Who is right?
   A. Technician A only
   B. Technician B only
   C. Both A and B
   D. Neither A or B

4. The drive axles on a truck with a walking beam suspension are out of alignment in a manner that is causing vehicle tire wear and steering instability. Technician A says the cause could be that the torque rods are too long or too short. Technician B says the cause could be worn walking beam bushings. Who is right?
   A. Technician A only
   B. Technician B only
   C. Both A and B
   D. Neither A or B

5. The driver of a truck says that it is too hard to steer and that the steering wheel return is too fast. Which of these is the most likely cause?
   A. too much negative caster
   B. too much positive caster
   C. too much negative camber
   D. too much positive camber

6. A steering gear binds when turning to the left after it has been adjusted. The most likely cause is that the:
   A. worm bearing preload was set too high
   B. steering shaft U-joints are sticking
   C. gearbox was not centered when the lash was adjusted
   D. recirculating ball nut thrust adjustment is off

Training for Certification

Prepare yourself for ASE testing with these questions on MEDIUM/HEAVY-DUTY TRUCK SUSPENSION AND STEERING

7. Which of these is most likely to cause steering wheel shimmy?
   A. too much positive caster
   B. out-of-balance wheels
   C. air in the power steering system
   D. low tire pressure

8. Technician A says that steering columns are collapsible to prevent the column from causing serious injury to the driver during a collision. Technician B says that when a steering column has been collapsed, the entire column must be replaced. Who is right?
   A. Technician A only
   B. Technician B only
   C. Both A and B
   D. Neither A or B

9. A constant buzzing noise comes from the power steering pump. Technician A says the cause could be air in the system. Technician B says the cause could be that the relief valve is stuck in the open position. Who is right?
   A. Technician A only
   B. Technician B only
   C. Both A and B
   D. Neither A or B

10. The steering gear sector shaft preload is to be set. Technician A says the steering wheel must be in the center position. Technician B says the drag link should be disconnected from the pitman arm. Who is right?
    A. Technician A only
    B. Technician B only
    C. Both A and B
    D. Neither A or B

11. Which of these could cause the front tires of a truck to show a feather-edged wear pattern?
    A. a wrong toe-in setting
    B. a wrong camber setting
    C. a wrong caster setting
    D. wrong tire pressure

12. The driver of a new truck says that he feels a light tire thump. Technician A says the cause could be an out-of-balance tire. Technician B says the cause could be an over-inflated tire. Who is right?
    A. Technician A only
    B. Technician B only
    C. Both A and B
    D. Neither A or B

13. A vehicle has exhibited power steering fluid leakage. Disassembly of components has revealed deteriorated seals in both the pump and steering gear. Technician A says to find out if the vehicle has been run severely overloaded. Technician B says to check for use of an incorrect replacement hose. Who is right?
    A. Technician A only
    B. Technician B only
    C. Both A and B
    D. Neither A or B

14. During inspection of a tire, a technician finds a slight bulge in one area of the tread. The next step taken should be:
    A. Remove the tire from the rim and seal the inner liner (the bulge probably results from an air leak).
    B. Replace the tire as its use is in violation of CVSA regulations and would put the truck out of service if it were subjected to a roadside inspection.
    C. Have the tire retreaded.
    D. Measure the size of the bulge to see if it is no greater than 3/8 inch and look for a small, blue triangle stamped into the tire nearby.

15. Technician A says that when diagnosing a power steering leak, the wheels should be in a straight-ahead position. Technician B says that when diagnosing a power steering leak, the steering wheel should be rotated from stop-to-stop to put pressure on the system. Who is right?
    A. Technician A only
    B. Technician B only
    C. Both A and B
    D. Neither A or B

Prepare yourself for ASE testing with these questions on MEDIUM/HEAVY-DUTY TRUCK SUSPENSION AND STEERING

16. A truck's leaf springs have broken at a low mileage. A careful inspection reveals no problems related to the spring system, such as frozen shackle bushings or worn hangers, bushings or spring pins. The truck has not been run overloaded. Technician A says the problem may have occurred because the U-bolt nuts were not retorqued at specified intervals after the springs were replaced. Technician B says the whole problem could be re-use of old U-bolts or installation of an inferior type of U-bolt. Who is right?
   A. Technician A only
   B. Technician B only
   C. Both A and B
   D. Neither A or B

17. A truck exhibits a strange combination of symptoms. The drive axles exhibit chronic seal wear problems. At the same time, there is some evidence of irregular drive axle tire wear. There is no evidence of driveshaft imbalance or worn driveshaft parts. The MOST likely cause of the problem is:
   A. driver abuse of the truck by frequently popping the clutch in very low gears on a steep upgrade
   B. severe imbalance of the drive axle tires and wheels
   C. worn shock absorbers on the tandem drive axle suspension system
   D. worn bushings in the torque rods locating the drive axles

18. A truck has exhibited problems with spring leaf failure that can be explained by inadequate clamping force. During an inspection, a technician is having trouble deciding whether or not a particular spring stack is adequately clamped. He knows the fasteners are properly torqued, but suspects bad fasteners have been used and wants a quick way to determine whether or not attaching parts should be replaced to protect the springs from further problems. Technician A says that if the stack feels and looks tight and parts retain the required torque after a few miles of operation, the fasteners are working. Technician B says to rap the U-bolt with a brass hammer. If the bolt yields a ringing sound, torque is probably OK. If it yields a dull thud, it should be replaced. Who is right?
   A. Technician A only
   B. Technician B only
   C. Both A and B
   D. Neither A or B

19. A tractor with a single height control valve exhibits a ride height that is consistently too high. A brief inspection has revealed that the height control valve is in reasonable mechanical condition and properly adjusted. Technician A says to check the air brake system operating pressure and make sure it is not too high. Technician B says to check the physical condition of all the shock absorbers as well as all the travel stops that may be incorporated in the suspension. Who is right?
   A. Technician A only
   B. Technician B only
   C. Both A and B
   D. Neither A or B

20. A truck fleet has had repeated tire blowouts. Technician A says they should review their tire changing procedures to make sure the proper tire changing tools and sealing solvents are being used. Technician B says they should review their repair procedures and make sure they are sealing a tire's inner liner when a puncture occurs. Who is right?
   A. Technician A only
   B. Technician B only
   C. Both A and B
   D. Neither A or B

21. A technician has been asked by a customer if he can get more even tire wear, and thereby improve tire life, by rotating the eight tires on the tandem drive axles of his tractor. Technician A says all the tires endure practically identical stresses and wear patterns. Technician B says irregular wear patterns will be canceled out. Who is right?
   A. Technician A only
   B. Technician B only
   C. Both A and B
   D. Neither A or B

22. When checking the front-end alignment on a truck, it is necessary to add _____ and _____ to get the included angle:
   A. kingpin inclination and toe-in
   B. caster and camber
   C. kingpin inclination and camber
   D. toe-in and caster

Prepare yourself for ASE testing with these questions on MEDIUM/HEAVY-DUTY TRUCK SUSPENSION AND STEERING

23. Which of these is the LEAST likely cause of too much front tire wear?
    A. underinflated tires
    B. out-of-balance tires
    C. a wrong toe-in setting
    D. a wrong caster setting

24. All of these must be checked before aligning the front wheels on a truck **EXCEPT**:
    A. tire pressure
    B. trim height
    C. wheel bearing adjustment
    D. tire balance

25. The driver of a truck with power steering says that it takes too much effort to steer. Any of these could be the cause **EXCEPT**:
    A. too low a power steering fluid level
    B. front-end out-of-alignment
    C. too much steering gear backlash
    D. a sticking relief valve

26. A truck with air suspension repeatedly exhibits shock breakage. All of these are items that should be checked **EXCEPT**:
    A. Check the part numbers of the shocks and make sure they are correct for the vehicle.
    B. Check the function of the ride height control valve.
    C. Check the torque of the shock mounting bolts.
    D. Check to make sure the vehicle's tire pressures are not excessively high.

27. A truck steers to the right practically all the time. All of the following are probable causes that should be checked out **EXCEPT**:
    A. incorrect caster setting
    B. incorrect camber setting
    C. loose suspension components
    D. malfunctioning brake slack adjuster

28. The vehicle's suspension system must do all of the following **EXCEPT**:
    A. support the load
    B. articulate the load (that is, maintain alignment during up-and-down motion)
    C. remove excess energy that otherwise becomes stored up in the springs and prevents smooth ride
    D. provide a rigid foundation for frame or trailer support

29. Which of the following is NOT a characteristic of air suspension:
    A. The ride is smoother when the truck runs empty.
    B. is more often used on drive and trailer axles than on the front axle
    C. does not provide much roll stiffness (allows the vehicle to lean more in turns than springs)
    D. has springs that usually last a long time

30. All of the following basic principles apply to sound leaf spring suspension repair procedures **EXCEPT**:
    A. If a truck has run for a long time with a broken spring leaf, replace the entire set.
    B. Never retorque the nuts that fasten U-bolts because this will stretch the bolts excessively (they were stretched to their limit during initial torque, if it was properly done).
    C. If a single leaf in a set of long front springs breaks, replace the entire set, even if you think you've caught the problem promptly.
    D. Never re-use U-bolts because they stretch during normal initial torque.

31. A truck's power steering pump has an internal failure. The power steering fluid has been checked and no signs of discoloring or contamination have been found. Technician A says after the pump is replaced, any type of power steering fluid is acceptable to use in the system. Technician B says after replacing the pump, the system should be flushed. Who is right?
    A. Technician A only
    B. Technician B only
    C. Both A and B
    D. Neither A or B

Prepare yourself for ASE testing with these questions on MEDIUM/HEAVY-DUTY TRUCK SUSPENSION AND STEERING

32. A technician is replacing a truck's kingpins. He has measured the kingpin bores and found them to be over the manufacturer's specifications. What should he do next?
    A. discard the axle
    B. install shims
    C. check to see if oversized kingpins are available
    D. none of the above

33. Technician A says that camber on a truck should be slightly positive. Technician B says that negative camber compensates for the normal deflection of the axle and front suspension joints. Who is right?
    A. Technician A only
    B. Technician B only
    C. Both A and B
    D. Neither A or B

34. A technician plans to replace tires on a truck with normal tire tread wear. He has inspected the suspension and steering systems and no defects have been found. After he has replaced the tires, what should he do with the old tire casings?
    A. have the casings retreaded
    B. discard the casings
    C. use them on an off-road truck
    D. use them on a trailer

35. A truck's frame is being inspected, and a crack has been found in the side rail that is moving toward the bottom flange around the radius of the rail. According to CVSA Out of Service Criteria, the crack should be no longer than:
    A. 2-in.
    B. 3½ -in.
    C. 3¼ -in.
    D. 1½ -in.

36. Technician A says that when a kingpin is found to be loose, it can be adjusted. Technician B says that lubricating the kingpin will only temporarily solve the problem. Who is right?
    A. Technician A only
    B. Technician B only
    C. Both A and B
    D. Neither A or B

37. Technician A says that hub piloted wheels and their hardware CANNOT be used on an axle with stud piloted wheels. Technician B says that on dual wheels, hub piloted wheels and stud piloted wheels CAN be mixed. Who is right?
    A. Technician A only
    B. Technician B only
    C. Both A and B
    D. Neither A or B

38. Tire tread depth in two adjacent tread grooves should not be less than:
    A. 1/32-in.
    B. 3/32-in.
    C. 2/32-in.
    D. 3/64-in.

39. All of the following will cause excessive steering looseness **EXCEPT**:
    A. sector shaft adjustment loose
    B. worn linkage
    C. excessive gear worm end-play
    D. loose power steering belt

40. Technician A says radial runout on cast spoke wheels can be adjusted by loosening and retorquing the rim clamps. Technician B says to adjust runout on disc wheels, the tire must be separated from the rim and rotated 180 degrees. Who is right?
    A. Technician A only
    B. Technician B only
    C. Both A and B
    D. Neither A or B

41. It is recommended to retorque wheel studs and nuts after:
    A. 100-200 miles
    B. 50-100 miles
    C. 300-350 miles
    D. never

42. Steering wheel free-play for a 16-in. steering wheel should be:
    A. 6⅜ inches
    B. 6¾ inches
    C. 5⅜ inches
    D. 5½ inches

Training for Certification

Prepare yourself for ASE testing with these questions on MEDIUM/HEAVY-DUTY TRUCK SUSPENSION AND STEERING

43. Which of the following is the **LEAST** likely to cause chronic spring breakage:
    A. seized shackle bushings
    B. worn spring hangers
    C. loose kingpins
    D. improper U-bolt torque

44. Technician A says when a single wheel stud is cracked or damaged, the vehicle can run without replacing the stud. Technician B says if a single wheel stud is cracked or damaged, all studs on that wheel should be replaced. Who is right?
    A. Technician A only
    B. Technician B only
    C. Both A and B
    D. Neither A or B

45. All of the following characteristics describe a remote mounted power steering reservoir **EXCEPT**:
    A. mounted inside the engine compartment
    B. mounted higher than the power steering pump
    C. vented to the atmosphere
    D. sealed with an O-ring or gasket

46. What is the meaning of the acronym DIP?
    A. diagnose, install, position
    B. drive, inspect, pressure
    C. deflate, inspect, protect
    D. none of the above

47. Technician A says the air-assist safety valve should cut off steering assist when the dash mounted reservoir air pressure gauge drops to 60-65 psi. Technician B says that turning the adjustment screw counterclockwise will lower the valve's cutoff point. Who is right?
    A. Technician A only
    B. Technician B only
    C. Both A and B
    D. Neither A or B

48. While driving down a smooth straight road, a truck driver says that it is hard to keep the truck going in a straight line. What is the **LEAST** likely cause?
    A. lack of lubrication in the steering gear
    B. steering gear loose at the frame mounting
    C. pitman arm loose at the steering gear
    D. excessive air pressure in the tires

49. Technician A says a power steering cooler helps to keep the fluid temperatures low in normal operating situations. Technician B says a power steering cooler will keep the system from overheating in the event of a failure. Who is right?
    A. Technician A only
    B. Technician B only
    C. Both A and B
    D. Neither A or B

50. What is the maximum deflection of the front axle when a technician is bending it to achieve a correct camber reading?
    A. ¼ inch
    B. ½ inch
    C. ⅜ inch
    D. ¾ inch

51. Leaf springs are divided into which of the following categories?
    A. tri-point and dual-point
    B. single-point and dual-point
    C. dual-point and variable rate
    D. constant-rate and tri-point

52. A truck with dual wheels comes into the shop with one inner tire that is flat. Technician A says the tire must be repaired or replaced before leaving. Technician B says the scrubbing of the tire along the road could cause a fire. Who is right?
    A. Technician A only
    B. Technician B only
    C. Both A and B
    D. Neither A or B

53. Technician A says that toe-in counteracts positive camber. Technician B says as parts wear, toe-in increases. Who is right?
    A. Technician A only
    B. Technician B only
    C. Both A and B
    D. Neither A or B

Prepare yourself for ASE testing with these questions on MEDIUM/HEAVY-DUTY TRUCK SUSPENSION AND STEERING

54. Technician A says that fifth wheel stops keep the trailer pin from sliding inside the fifth wheel. Technician B says some trucks have an air-operated fifth wheel locking control. Who is right?
    A. Technician A only
    B. Technician B only
    C. Both A and B
    D. Neither A or B

55. When servicing a steering column, the first thing a technician should do is:
    A. adjust toe
    B. raise and safely support the vehicle
    C. deactivate the SRS circuit
    D. drain the power steering fluid

56. The component designed to fit into the pintle hook is called a:
    A. cross bar
    B. drawback bar
    C. towing bar
    D. drawbar

57. Technician A says the pitman arm is the strongest arm in the steering linkage system. Technician B says the pitman arm is mounted on the steering gear input shaft and is secured by a large nut. Who is right?
    A. Technician A only
    B. Technician B only
    C. Both A and B
    D. Neither A or B

58. Technician A says that the up-and-down motion of leaf springs is dampened by air bags. Technician B says shock absorbers transfer heat through friction. Who is right?
    A. Technician A only
    B. Technician B only
    C. Both A and B
    D. Neither A or B

59. Runout is defined as:
    A. the up-and-down or side-to-side movement of the axle.
    B. the up-and-down or side-to-side movement of the steering.
    C. the up-and-down or side-to-side movement of the tire or wheel.
    D. none of the above

60. Technician A says that toe-out-on-turns means that the inside wheel of the vehicle tracks a much larger circle than the outside wheel. Technician B says the relative position of the steering arm joints to the kingpin centerline causes toe-out-on-turns. Who is right?
    A. Technician A only
    B. Technician B only
    C. Both A and B
    D. Neither A or B

61. The flexible couplings attached to steering columns are typically called:
    A. rib joints
    B. rag joints
    C. rack joints
    D. damper joints

62. Technician A makes toe-in corrections first when aligning a vehicle. Technician B says toe-in is the amount the rear of the front wheels are closer together than the front of the front wheels. Who is right?
    A. Technician A only
    B. Technician B only
    C. Both A and B
    D. Neither A or B

63. Torque arms are designed to:
    A. keep the axle from twisting
    B. keep the frame from twisting
    C. keep suspension jounce at a minimum
    D. keep the steering from pulling

64. Which of the following are characteristics of a kingpin?
    A. can be tapered or straight
    B. connects pitman arm to steering linkage
    C. cannot be lubricated
    D. is located in the steering gear

Training for Certification

Prepare yourself for ASE testing with these questions on MEDIUM/HEAVY-DUTY TRUCK SUSPENSION AND STEERING

65. The correct term for an axle that is moved slightly to the rear is:
    A. push back
    B. knuckle back
    C. set back
    D. load back

66. Technician A says loose U-bolts will cause the axle to shift. Technician B says when a spring is replaced, the old U-bolts can be reused as long as they are inspected and retorqued in accordance with the vehicle's maintenance schedule. Who is right?
    A. Technician A only
    B. Technician B only
    C. Both A and B
    D. Neither A or B

67. A truck that is being aligned exhibits inaccurate Ackerman geometry from one side to another and is grossly out of specification. Technician A says the problem could be a bent steering arm. Technician B says Ackerman geometry is also known as toe-out steering radius. Who is right?
    A. Technician A only
    B. Technician B only
    C. Both A and B
    D. Neither A or B

68. What organization is charged with rating replacement U-bolts?
    A. STS
    B. ASE
    C. SAE
    D. TMC

69. An alternate procedure to inspect steering linkage for looseness is called:
    A. steering link check
    B. steering movement check
    C. dry park check
    D. lock-to-lock check

70. Which one of the following is a characteristic of semi-integral power steering gears?
    A. uses a control valve
    B. needs more effort to steer
    C. is self-contained
    D. none of the above

71. The lower steering shaft U-joint has been replaced on a medium duty truck. While parking the vehicle, the driver notices that the steering is binding when turning the steering wheel from stop to stop. Technician A says the steering shaft U-joints are incorrectly phased. Technician B says that this is this symptom is the winding and unwinding of the steering shaft called Torsional Imbalance. Who is right?
    A. Technician A
    B. Technician B
    C. Both A and B
    D. Neither A or B

72. Technician A says to begin checking the cab height control valve operation, the linkage should be connected to the valve and the air should be exhausted from the system. Technician B says slight leakage from the height control valve when it is in the neutral position is acceptable. Who is right?
    A. Technician A
    B. Technician B
    C. Both A and B
    D. Neither A or B

73. Technician A says lift axles are auxiliary drive axles that help to support additional vehicle weight when needed. Technician B says self-steering lift axles allow for greater truck maneuverability and can be used longer. Who is right?
    A. Technician A
    B. Technician B
    C. Both A and B
    D. Neither A or B

74. Technician A says static balancing is preferred over dynamic balancing. Technician B says material can be inserted into the tire before it is mounted onto the rim for the purpose of balancing the tire/wheel assembly.
    A. Technician A
    B. Technician B
    C. Both A and B
    D. Neither A or B

75. A truck is equipped with an air-assist steering system. The driver complains that the steering wheel is difficult to turn when maneuvering the vehicle in delivery applications. Technician A says the problem could be with the torque valve. Technician B says the problem could be with the power cylinder. Who is right?
    A. Technician A
    B. Technician B
    C. Both A and B
    D. Neither A or B

Notes

Answers to Study-Guide Test Questions

1. The correct answer is C, both technicians are right. Height control valves can fail in either direction—that is, by controlling the height at too great a level or at too low a level. If the truck leans, the cause can be either too great a height on one side or too low a height on the other. Until the technician knows that one side is too high or the other too low, he must assume that either valve might be malfunctioning.

2. The correct answer is C, both technicians are right. Either a worn shackle bushing or worn shock bushing can cause noise due to looseness when the truck hits a good bump. If there is clearance between the rubber bushing and mounting bolt, or if the rubber bushing has worn very thin, elongated or even broken and fallen out, the result will be a clattering noise as the motion of the suspension repeatedly takes up the clearance first in one direction and then in the other.

3. The correct answer is A. Correct caster is critically important in keeping tires at the right angle and enabling the steering system to maintain directional stability. Since the caster shims would have to be removed for this work to be done, it's quite logical to assume they might have been installed backwards, which would create the critically incorrect caster setting that would make the truck wander severely.

4. The correct answer is B. The beam bushings maintain horizontal alignment of the axles, especially on turns. When bushings are worn, the beam on either side can move forward or backward, turning the axles in relation to the frame and causing the type of misalignment that causes tire wear and steering problems.

5. The correct answer is B. Caster action is the most critical suspension alignment specification in terms of affecting steering wheel return to the center. Caster actually lifts the truck as the wheel is turned in either direction; when the driver allows the wheel to return to center, the weight of the truck actually forces the steering system to that position. When the caster setting is too high, the weight of the truck exerts too much force in centering the steering and creates the symptoms noted.

6. The correct answer is A. Excessive worm bearing preload would show up as binding as the steering was turned to one extreme and the friction became excessive due to the combination of normal load and too much preload. B is not the answer because sticking U-joints should be apparent and cause rough rotation of the wheel at all steering angles. If either lash or ball nut thrust adjustment was incorrect, the box would either bind at the center or be too loose at the extremes of travel.

7. The correct answer is B. Out-of-balance wheels cause a high frequency vibration, which shows up in the wheel as shimmy. A is not the answer because caster shows up as too much self-centering action (hard steering). Air in the power steering system causes constantly or intermittently hard steering (lack of hydraulic force). Low tire pressures generally do not cause an uneven force on the steering system, but rather poor tread contact with the road and vague steering or hard steering.

8. The correct answer is C, both technicians are right. Steering columns are made to be collapsible to prevent the column from seriously impacting the driver during a front-end collision. If an accident has occurred, and the steering column has partially collapsed, the entire column must be replaced.

9. The correct answer is A. Fluid passes through the power steering system parts at high flow rates and under high pressures. When it becomes aerated, the bubbles cause rough, uneven flow and consequent noise. When a relief valve sticks open, fluid flows more smoothly (in a less restricted manner than normal), causing no noise but poor power assist instead.

10. The correct answer is C, both technicians are right. The steering wheel must be in the center position because clearances in the box change (they are tightest at center) and setting preload at another position would cause binding at the center. The drag link must be disconnected because preload is measured by turning the steering box. It produces a very small amount of friction that must be measured with an inch pound torque wrench and is much smaller than the friction inherent in the rest of the steering system.

Answers to Study-Guide Test Questions

11. The correct answer is A. Toe-in that is incorrect causes the entire tread to contact the road at an angle; this is what produces feather-edge wear. Incorrect camber causes wear on one side of the tire because it contacts the road unevenly, from side-to-side, when camber is incorrect. C is not the answer because caster that is incorrectly set can produce poor steerability, but usually does not critically affect tire wear. Wrong tire pressures produce wear that is excessive at center or on both sides.

12. The correct answer is A. A tire that is out of balance produces uneven forces in the steering system. The tire tends to bounce up-and-down as the heavier portion alternately goes over the top and hits the pavement. Tires that are overinflated still produce constant forces on the steering system. Overinflation tends to create uneven wear and may cause imprecise steering because the full width of the tread does not contact the road surface.

13. The correct answer is C, both technicians are right. The most likely cause of the problem is overheating of the fluid because all the seals in the system deteriorated. Running a vehicle severely overloaded or installing a hose with too small a diameter could overheat the power steering fluid and create widespread failure of the system's seals.

14. The correct answer is D. A bulge not exceeding 3/8-in. and marked by a blue triangle indicates that the tire is bulging not because of a structural defect but because of a section repair. The blue triangle merely indicates a repair has been made. A tire that has a bulge from a repair of a dimension within the 3/8-in. limit will pass a roadside inspection without any problem and will operate safely.

15. The correct answer is B. When diagnosing a power steering leak, the area should be clean and the system should be full of power steering fluid. The engine should be started and the steering wheel rotated from stop-to-stop, making sure the wheel is not held against either stop for more than two seconds.

16. The correct answer is C, both technicians are right. Leaf spring stacks are extremely sensitive to proper mounting. They naturally tend to settle especially shortly after being installed. U-bolts must be of extremely high quality to retain torque adequately. Thus, the best procedure would be to replace the U-bolts with an approved part, torque the nuts to specification and be sure to retorque them at specified intervals.

17. The correct answer is D. Worn bushings in the torque rods are causing the drive axles to sometimes run with their mounting angles incorrect. This, in turn, is causing the symptoms because the driveshafts sometimes operate at excessive angles. This excessive angularity causes vibration, which eventually reaches the seals and destroys them. Also, incorrect operating position causes the tires in the tandem setup to track improperly (work against each other), causing the symptoms noted. Popping the clutch frequently would be more likely to produce twisted or worn driveshafts and rapid tire wear as opposed to irregular wear. Severe imbalance, although it would wear the tires irregularly, would not tend to impact the seals. Worn shocks might cause tire wear if they were almost completely ineffective, but they would not likely cause a seal problem.

18. The correct answer is B. Pull-around torque or the torque required to turn a fastener is not always an indicator of clamping force. On the other hand, a U-bolt that exhibits a ringing sound is probably under sufficient tension to hold the stack secure, while one that exhibits a dull thud is not tight enough.

19. The correct answer is B. The shocks and travel stops are probably not working properly. Even with a high brake air system pressure, the control valve will shut off tight, sealing even with excessive pressure at the proper ride height. On the other hand, if suspension travel is excessive in the downward direction, this can allow the truck to ride at too low a height for a brief period over hard bumps. This tricks the control valve into feeding air to the system when it is not actually needed.

20. The correct answer is C, both technicians are right. Either improper tire changing procedures or such incorrect repair procedures as failure to seal the inner liner can result in insidious damage and a blowout down the road.

Answers to Study-Guide Test Questions

21. The correct answer is B. Tread wear is uneven on tandem drive axles for two reasons: First, the distribution of power is not perfectly equal between all the wheel positions and rotation will equal out the variations. Second, when a tandem axle tractor takes a corner, the forward axle's tires scrub a bit more than those on the rear axle; rotation equalizes this wear, too.

22. The correct answer is C. This is because this sum gives the relationship between the centerline of the wheel and the centerline of the kingpin (or knuckle support pivots with lighter duty type front axles). This angle is built into the knuckle forging and remains constant unless the spindle is damaged during use. Toe-in and caster do not have any effect on this angle.

23. The correct answer is D. Caster does not affect the way the tread contacts the road or cause the tire to scrub down the road at an angle. Underinflation forces the edges of the tire to take most of the load, concentrating wear, as well as producing excessive flexing (squirming) of the tread and consequent wear. Tires that are out of balance focus wear where the heavier portion of the tire slaps against the road. Toe-in makes the tread scrub across the road, causing featheredge wear.

24. The correct answer is D. Tire balance is the only one of the four factors that does not affect alignment readings. An unbalanced tire will still hold the vehicle at the right height, and sit at the same angle to the vehicle as an unbalanced tire. Tire pressure affects ride height and, therefore, can affect the angle between the frame (and front axle) and the ground. This, in turn, affects the angle of the kingpins, which is what determines caster. Trim height affects frame angle and will affect alignment just as incorrect tire pressures will. Wheel bearing adjustment that is incorrect will change the angle between the wheel and frame and, therefore, affect alignment readings.

25. The correct answer is C. Excessive backlash in the steering gear reduces operating friction in the steering box and will therefore only make the vehicle easier to steer. The symptom associated with excessive backlash would be vague steering. Low fluid level will tend to aerate the fluid and deprive the power system of hydraulic force, making for hard steering. Front end alignment factors that are incorrect will increase steering effort considerably (often by increasing caster action). A sticking relief valve will usually cause bypass of fluid pressure, depriving the power steering gear of necessary hydraulic pressure, making the system behave almost like manual steering.

26. The correct answer is D. Though high tire pressures might make the vehicle ride harshly, they are not known to create sufficient stress on the shocks to break them. Misapplied shocks might break due to inadequate travel or insufficient capacity to keep the suspension system operating in a stable manner. The ride height control valve should be checked because an incorrect ride height could cause the shock to constantly hit the upper or lower limit of its travel. Mounting bolt torque should be checked because excessive torque could pinch the shock bushings, prevent them from allowing the shock to rotate freely as necessary, and so put excessive stress on the body of the shock.

27. The correct answer is C. Loose suspension components might cause the truck to steer off course, but the effect would come and go as suspension play developed and went away as the truck went over bumps. Caster and camber are alignment settings that, if incorrect, would constantly hold the wheel at an incorrect angle for straight steering. A malfunctioning auto slack adjuster, if it consistently adjusted up too tight, would cause the brake on one side to constantly increase the rolling resistance for that one wheel. This, in turn, would cause the vehicle to steer to one side unless the operator compensated with the wheel.

28. The correct answer is D. The suspension system is, by nature, not rigid, as a rigid system would transfer all the energy generated as the wheels run over bumps to the frame and the load. Even systems designed to support extreme loads at least incorporate rubber cushioning. The system must obviously support the load, keep the vehicle's axles and frame in appropriate alignment for safe steering and level support, and remove excess energy (with shock absorbers)

29. The correct answer is C. Air suspension gives excellent roll stiffness because the supporting springs are not also used to control articulation— that is left to separate blades and hinge-type joints. The height control valve reduces air pressure, softening the springs, when the vehicle is unloaded. Front axles carry a more constant weight and therefore benefit less from

Answers to Study-Guide Test Questions

the ability of air suspension to adjust for weight. Air springs are so flexible that they tend not to be subjected to fatigue. Also, the air springs are not stressed if suspension parts begin to lose their freedom of operation due to imperfect maintenance.

30. The correct answer is B. Two retorquings are typically required. Retorquing simply restores the bolt to its optimum stretch as the spring stack settles. All the other principles are known means of helping the technician give the vehicle owner a lasting repair. All of them relate to catching excessive stress, which is created when there is a failure because the spring suspension behaves as a system, not a collection of individual parts.

31. The correct answer is D, neither technician is right. Always use the type of power steering fluid specified by the vehicle manufacturer since fluid requirements may vary from one vehicle to another. Component failure can result if fluids are mixed once a specific type is established. Only if it is necessary to change the type of fluid, or the fluid becomes contaminated or discolored, is the entire system to be flushed.

32. The correct answer is C. Once the kingpin bores are found to be oversized, the bore can be reamed to allow installation of an oversized kingpin—if manufacturer's specifications say that this is an option. Only if oversized kingpins are not an option should the axle be replaced.

33. The correct answer is A. Trucks typically run a slight, positive camber with the vehicle off the front wheels. It is positive camber that compensates for the normal deflection of the axle and front suspension joints as the front suspension is loaded, not negative camber.

34. The correct answer is A. Basic tire designs share a common casing. When tread is worn, the casing can be retreaded with a different type tread and used in a different wheel position. It can also be used in a different geographic section of the country, where traction requirements are different or as required by the customer. The technician can send the casings to a certified retreading facility to have new treads installed. While tread wears relatively rapidly and lasts only a year or two (100,000 to, at maximum, 200,000 miles), the casing itself—the tire's basic structure—is an extremely expensive, durable and reusable item.

35. The correct answer is D. When there is a crack of 1½-in. or longer in the frame side rail that is directed toward the bottom of flange around the radius of the rail, the vehicle can be placed out of service at a roadside inspection.

36. The correct answer is B. Lubricating the kingpins will help eliminate some play, but only temporarily. Excessive play in the kingpins can only be remedied by replacing the kingpins and bushings.

37. The correct answer is A. Hub piloted disc wheels are centered on the wheel hub by means of indents built into the hub assembly. The center hole of the disc rests on these indents and centers the wheel. Two-piece flange nuts make contact with the face of the disc at the stud hole. There is no ball seat at the stud hole, since the flange nuts tighten flat against the disc wheel. Stud piloted disc wheels use the securing nuts to center the wheel onto the hub assembly. These wheels have a ball seat at the stud hole, and wheel centering occurs when the securing nuts are tightened in the proper fashion. Although they may have the same bolt hole patterns, don't mix hub piloted disc wheels and their hardware with stud piloted disc wheels. Damage to wheels or studs, and possible wheel loss can result.

38. The correct answer is C. Measurement of the tire tread depth in two adjacent tread grooves should not be less than 2/32-in.

39. The correct answer is D. A steering gear shaft adjusted too loose, worn steering linkage, or excessive steering gear worm end-play will cause the steering to seem loose. A loose power steering belt will impede power assist and cause the steering to be hard.

40. The correct answer is C, both technicians are right. Radial runout can be checked on cast spoke wheels by loosening and retorquing the rim clamp nuts according to manufacturer's procedures. On disc wheels, the tire must be deflated and rotated 180 degrees to achieve proper runout.

Training for Certification

Answers to Study-Guide Test Questions

41. The correct answer is B. Retorquing a short time after installation (50 to 100 miles) to ensure full seating is important. Retorquing at an appropriate interval even when wheels are not removed is also an important adjunct to operating safety. Consult the manufacturer for torque specifications and procedures and retorquing mileage intervals.

42. The correct answer is B. When troubleshooting a power steering gear, check the steering wheel play against CVSA allowable maximums. The movement measured in inches for a 16-in. steering wheel is 6¾ inches.

43. The correct answer is C. Although kingpins are a critical part of the suspension system, loose kingpins would not cause chronic spring breakage.

44. The correct answer is B. The technician should check the stud nuts for cracks, abnormal wear and stripped threads. Should a single stud be broken or damaged, the entire group of studs should be replaced to avoid future failure that may not be apparent during an examination of the studs or nuts.

45. The correct answer is D. The remote reservoir tank is mounted inside the engine compartment, and is located in a position that allows downward flow of fluid to the power steering pump. This creates a constant flow of fluid and decreases the chance of pump cavitation. Most reservoirs are vented to the atmosphere through an opening that lets air leave or enter the space above the oil as the oil level rises or falls. The pump mounted power steering reservoir is sealed to the power steering pump using an O-ring or gasket.

46. The correct answer is C. For the safety of the repairman, the acronym DIP should be remembered when working with tires and wheels. It stands for DEFLATE—the tire before working on it. INSPECT—the rim, rings, lug holes and tires for damage, including distortion and proper sealing. PROTECT—yourself by placing the tire and wheel assembly in an inflation cage before inflating.

47. The correct answer is C, both technicians are right. The air-assist safety valve should cut off steering assist when the dash mounted reservoir air pressure gauge drops to 60-65 psi. Turning the screw clockwise will raise the cutoff point; turning it counterclockwise will lower the cutoff point.

48. The correct answer is D. Excessive tire pressure usually causes a hard ride, excessive wheel bounce, and excessive center tread wear. When the vehicle darts out of a steered line or oversteers, the problem can be attributed to a poorly lubricated steering gear, loose steering gear mountings, or a loose pitman arm at the steering gear.

49. The correct answer is A. A power steering cooler keeps fluid temperatures low, promoting longer component life and reducing the potential for leaks in normal operating conditions. However, the cooler will not keep the lubricant temperatures low if there is another failure in the system that is causing fluid burn.

50. The correct answer is B. Although camber is not adjustable on most trucks, minor bending of a solid beam axle can correct some camber alignment problems if the bends are made by qualified personnel. However, these adjustments are not recommended by most vehicle manufacturers. The bends may deflect the axle up to approximately 1/2-in. and should be done cold with special equipment. Do not apply heat to the axle in order to bend it as that portion could be weakened.

51. The correct answer is B. Leaf spring suspensions are divided into two basic categories: Single- and dual-point. Single-point types use a beam that has bushings on both ends. The spring uses front and rear hangers. Torque rods locate the axles laterally. Dual-point types have four springs instead of two. An equalizer allows a degree of articulation between the axles in some designs.

52. The correct answer is C, both technicians are right. A truck with a flat on one of its dual wheels must have the tire repaired immediately. The 'cardinal sin' is running dual wheels with one tire flat, which causes critical overheating of the tire carrying the entire load. This may even cause the flat tire to catch on fire due to scrubbing the tread along the road.

53. The correct answer is A. Toe-in performs the function of preloading steering linkage joints and counteracts the wheel's tendency to pull outward at the front due to positive camber. As the required camber increases, generally so does the toe-in. Note that toe-in decreases as parts wear.

Answers to Study-Guide Test Questions

54. The correct answer is B. Fifth wheel stops keep the fifth wheel from sliding from the mounting bracket assembly. These stops are welded to the fifth wheel mounting bracket at all four corners. Some tractors are equipped with an air control to unlock the fifth wheel. This control allows the driver to unlock the fifth wheel from the cab, using a dash-mounted valve.

55. The correct answer is C. Before servicing the steering column, make sure the Supplemental Restraint System (SRS) air bag module circuit is fully deactivated. Follow the vehicle manufacturer's recommended procedure to deactivate and remove the air bag module. Always wear safety glasses.

56. The correct answer is D. The drawbar is designed to fit into the pintle hook, and is used to pull double trailer, triple trailer and truck-trailer combinations. It is important to use a mounting structure on the trailer of sufficient strength to support the rated capacity of the drawbar. Also, the mounting surface must have an adequate chamfer to clear the drawbar shank fillet so that the drawbar is flush with its mounting surface.

57. The correct answer is A. The pitman arm is the strongest arm in the steering linkage system. It is made of steel and designed to accept the turning motion of the steering gear output shaft and transfer that motion into the torque needed to move the rest of the steering linkage back-and-forth. It is splined to the steering gear output shaft and secured to the shaft by a large nut.

58. The correct answer is B. The up-and-down motion of the leaf spring is dampened by shock absorbers, which contain hydraulic fluid or gas, and pistons with seals in a cylinder. The energy that would otherwise perpetuate the jounce is converted to heat through friction.

59. The correct answer is C. Runout is the up-and-down (radial) and side-to-side (lateral) movement of the tire or wheel when it is rotating. A tire or wheel that is out of round or not running true cannot only contribute to driver discomfort and increased operating costs, it can be a safety concern.

60. The correct answer is B. When a truck is steered into a turn, the outside wheel of the vehicle tracks a much larger circle than the inside wheel. Therefore, the outside wheel must be steered to a somewhat less acute angle than the inside wheel. This difference in angle is often called toe-out-on-turns. The change in angle from toe-in, in the straight-ahead position, to toe-out in the turn, is caused by the relative positions of the steering arm joints to the kingpin centerline and to each other.

61. The correct answer is B. Most steering columns include U-joints or flexible couplings (flexible couplings are typically called rag joints). Normally, a worn or damaged joint can be easily replaced. Most flex couplings are replaceable or rebuildable, and kits are available, but some flexible couplings are fixed parts of the column shaft and can't be replaced separately.

62. The correct answer is D, neither technician is right. Since toe-in is affected by caster and camber, it should be the last adjustment made. Toe-in is the amount that the front of the front wheels are closer together than they are at the back of the front wheels.

63. The correct answer is A. Torque arms keep the axle from twisting under the chassis in reaction to torque load from the drivetrain. Movement from side-to-side due to worn torque rod parts will overload the suspension system, resulting in premature wear or even failure of parts.

64. The correct answer is A. The kingpin or knuckle pin secures the steering knuckle to the axle. It can be either tapered or straight, depending on the manufacturer. Inspection and lubrication of the kingpin must be performed in accordance with the manufacturer's recommended service procedures.

65. The correct answer is C. Front axles on many trucks have been moved slightly to the rear (or set back) as regulations regarding overall truck length have changed. This has provided longer, smoother riding springs and improved front tire life. The latter has happened because those tires are more consistently loaded and less likely to develop uneven tread wear.

Answers to Study-Guide Test Questions

66. The correct answer is A. Loose axle U-bolts will allow the axle to shift on the springs. Never reuse U-bolts because of the stretching that occurs during normal initial torque, and the impossibility of getting effective clamping force or pull-up torque when they are retorqued.

67. The correct answer is C, both technicians are right. If the front-end angles, including toe-in, are set correctly, and the toe-out is found to be grossly different or incorrect, one or both of the steering arms are bent. Ackerman geometry is also known as toe-out or toe-out steering radius. When a truck is steered into a turn, the outside wheel of the vehicle tracks a much larger circle than the inside wheel. Therefore, the outside wheel must be steered to a somewhat less acute angle than the inside wheel. This change in angle from toe-in in the straight-ahead position to toe-out in the turn is caused by the relative position of the steering arm joints to the kingpin centerline and to each other

68. The correct answer is C. The Society of Automotive Engineers (SAE) grade of bolt is critical. Some manufacturers recommend at least a Grade 7 bolt (115,000 psi yield strength) for highway trucks and Grade 8 (130,000 psi) for off-road. It is important to heed manufacturer's recommendations as to U-bolt replacement and grade.

69. The correct answer is C. The steering linkage can also be inspected using a procedure called a 'dry park check.' With the engine off, have an assistant rotate the steering wheel from side-to-side while you inspect the steering linkage joints for looseness. Any side-to-side movement of the steering linkage joints is cause for replacement.

70. The correct answer is A. Semi-integral units provide hydraulic assistance to the steering unit with the use of a control valve, mounted in conjunction with a manual-type steering gear. The integral steering gear assemblies are self-contained hydraulic units, with the hydraulic pressure developed by an independently-mounted fluid pump driven by the engine.

71. The correct answer is A. When U-joints are replaced, they must be phased in order to eliminate Torsional Excitation, or winding and unwinding of the steering shaft. U-joint phasing is the relative position of one yoke to another within a 360-degree revolution. Most U-joint yokes and slip joints are match marked as to be installed 180-degrees from each other. An incorrectly phased shaft will cause the shaft to bind, producing premature wear of components.

72. The correct answer is D, neither technician. When checking the cab height control valve, the linkage must be disconnected from the valve and the air system must be built up to manufacturer's specifications. After the linkage is disconnected, operate the valve in both directions and observe the cab raising and lowering. If the height control valve has air leaks after it has returned to the neutral position, suspect a defective valve.

73. The correct answer is B. Some lift axles are self-steering, which allows for greater truck maneuverability for longer periods when the lift axle is lowered. Lift axles are not however drive axles, and are non-powered. Their only function is to assist in handling increased truck loads.

74. The correct answer is D, neither technician. Dynamic balancing is the preferred method if long tire life and smooth operation are to be achieved. However, it must be repeated at regular intervals if normal changes in balance are to be corrected. Certain types of materials are marketed for the purpose of balancing the tire by installing a fine grain or liquid material, but they must be installed inside the tire via the valve stem.

75. The correct answer is C, both technicians. The torque valve senses more than 10-lbs. pressure on the steering wheel (0.04-in. movement) by changing its length very slightly. This, in turn, meters air to a power cylinder. The power cylinder is fastened to the frame and applies force to the wheel arm or tie-rod to assist the driver in turning and holding the steering linkage.

Notes

Glossary of Terms

--a--

abrasion - rubbing away or wearing of a component.

absorb - to trap liquids or gases with an absorbent material.

acidity - acid quality or condition; in lubrication, the presence of acidic materials which cause corrosion, sludge and other contamination.

Ackerman geometry - also known as toe-out or toe-out steering radius. When a truck is steered into a turn, the outside wheel of the vehicle tracks a much larger circle than the inside wheel. Therefore, the outside wheel must be steered to a somewhat less acute angle than the inside wheel. This change in angle from toe-in in the straight-ahead position to toe-out in the turn is caused by the relative position of the steering arm joints to the kingpin centerline and to each other.

aeration - to expose to the air or mix with air, as with a liquid; to charge a liquid with gas.

air-assisted power steering - powered by the brake system's air compressor. It uses a torque valve to meter air to a power cylinder, depending upon the steering system's demands. The power cylinder is anchored to the frame and applies force to the wheel arm or tie-rod to assist the driver in turning and holding the steering linkage.

air bag (SRS) - actuated component of the supplemental restraint system developed for safety.

air compressor - engine-driven via a belt or direct gear, the compressor pressurizes the air tank to supply chassis suspension, cab suspension and certain accessories for operation.

air compressor cut-out - predetermined point at which the air governor halts compression of air by the compressor.

air governor - controls the compressor unloader mechanism and also maintains system air pressure between pre-determined minimum and maximum levels.

air spring - suspension device made up of a flexible bladder containing compressed air. The air spring takes the place of a conventional coil or leaf spring. Air is supplied by an on-board compressor, usually with auxiliary equipment to sense vehicle height and modify the pressure in the air spring as needed.

air suspension - system that relies on air springs instead of steel springs or hard-rubber mounts to adjust and control height and stability of cab and/or chassis.

air tank - main supply component in an air brake system that holds and distributes pressurized air to cab and chassis components.

alignment - an adjustment to bring parts or components into a line or proper coordination.

aluminum - lightweight nonferrous metal alloy.

articulate - the word articulate refers to controlling the motion that occurs in a suspension component in a precise way. Wear or breakage of parts that interfere with normal articulation causes problems elsewhere. For example, when rear axle locating torque arm bushings wear, driveshafts may wear because the axles do not articulate properly.

--b--

balance - condition of equal weight distribution within a component or among components; the act of equalizing the weight distribution, such as balancing a tire.

ball joint - suspension component that provides a pivot point, allowing the steering knuckle to move up-and-down as well as turn in response to steering input. The ball fits into a socket housing that is attached to the control arm and the stud on the other end of the ball is attached to the steering knuckle. A dust cover is installed over the ball and socket assembly to keep dirt out and lubricant in.

bead - steel reinforced inner edge of a tire, which fits inside and seals against the wheel rim.

bias-ply tires - bias-ply tires employ belts that run diagonally across each other. A belt leaves the bead on one side and runs to the opposite bead at an angle. This type construction proved stronger at a time when belt materials were not as durable as they are today. Bias tires are cheaper but give shorter life and poorer fuel economy than radial tires.

bump steer - steering problem in which a vehicle tends to the left or the right after a bump, without steering wheel input from the driver. This is usually caused by some steering misalignment or damage that permits change of toe when the suspension works up-and-down.

Glossary of Terms

--c--

camber - camber or camber angle is the amount of front wheel inclination either toward or away from a vertical line at the center of the vehicle. Camber is spoken of, and measured in, degrees from the true perpendicular. A wheel that is tilted outward at the top has positive camber; a wheel that is tilted inward at the top has negative camber. Trucks typically run a slight positive camber angle with the wheels off the ground to compensate for the normal deflection of the front axle and suspension joints as the suspension is loaded.

castellated nut - nut with slots through which a cotter pin can be passed to secure the nut to its bolt or stud.

castellations - slots cut in a bolt head or on nut flanges, through which a cotter pin is inserted to secure the fastener.

caster - caster or caster angle is the angle in degrees that the kingpin is tilted toward the front or back of the vehicle. Positive caster means that the top of the kingpin is tilted toward the back of the truck. Positive caster puts the point where the kingpin axis intersects with the road ahead of the tire contact point. Positive caster causes the truck's steering wheel to tend to return to the straight-ahead position when the steering wheel is released.

center link - steering linkage component that attaches the pitman arm to the idler arm, tie-rod or crosslink.

control arm - a suspension component that connects the vehicle frame to the steering knuckle or axle housing and allows the up-and-down movement of the wheels.

cords - the inner materials (usually fiberglass or steel) running through the plies that produce strength in a tire.

--d--

dampen - to slow or reduce oscillations or movement.

directional stability - the ability of a truck to travel in a straight line on a flat surface with a minimum of driver control.

directional tires - tires with a tread pattern that is designed to give maximum traction by removing water from under the tread in such a way as to minimize the risk of aquaplaning. Directional tires must be installed to turn in a specific direction.

dowel - peg or pin which fits into corresponding holes used for holding two parts together or to locate two parts in a set position.

drag link - steering linkage component that connects the pitman arm and the steering arm.

drawbar - the drawbar is designed to fit into the pintle hook, and is used to pull double trailer, triple trailer and truck-trailer combinations.

--e--

elasticity - having the property of immediately returning to original size, shape or position after being stretched, squeezed, flexed, expanded, etc.; the principle by which a bolt can be stretched a certain amount. Each time the stretching load is reduced, the bolt returns to exactly its original, normal size.

elastic limit - the point, as a bolt is stretched during torquing, past which it suddenly begins to be permanently deformed. A bolt could be repeatedly torqued to its elastic limit, loosened and retorqued, and would never lose its ability to hold that torque.

energy - capacity for doing work and overcoming resistance.

--f--

fifth wheel - device mounted to a tractor frame used to connect and secure a trailer.

fifth wheel height - distance from the ground or floor surface to the top of a fifth wheel when it is parallel to the ground.

fifth wheel plate - device that connects the trailer that houses the locking mechanism.

flow test - a test to ensure that a power steering pump can provide the required volume of fluid measured in units such as gallons per minute at full operating pressure. This is a vital test because a pump may be able to provide sufficient pressure but insufficient flow. A pump in this condition may provide inadequate power steering assist under some circumstances.

Training for Certification

Glossary of Terms

--g--

galling - weld-like damage to a metal due to lack of lubrication.

gear - toothed wheel, disc, etc. designed to mesh with another or with the thread of a worm; used to transfer or change motion.

gear pump - positive displacement pump that uses two meshing external gears, one drive and one driven.

--h--

hanger - mounting bracket that connects one end of a leaf spring to the truck frame.

heavy-duty truck - truck with a 26,001 lb. or more Gross Vehicle Weight (GVW).

height control valve - the height control valve detects the height of the frame above the axles mechanically-in effect, air spring height and degree of inflation. It feeds air from the air brake system into the air springs when height is too low and it exhausts air from the system when height is excessive.

height sensor - component used in an air suspension system to signal a control unit when the vehicle is riding low or high. In response to this signal, compressed air is either sent to or vented from the air springs.

--i--

idler arm - conventional steering system component consisting of an arm that swivels in a bushing on a shaft, which is attached to the frame. The idler arm is mounted on the right side of the vehicle and is the same length and set at the same angle as the pitman arm. Its function is to hold the right end of the centerlink level with the left end, which is moved by the pitman arm, and transfer the steering motion to the right side tie-rod.

included angle - a front axle alignment term consisting of the sum of kingpin inclination and camber. This sum gives the relationship between the centerline of the wheel and the centerline of the kingpin (or knuckle support pivots with lighter duty type front axles). This angle is built into the knuckle forging and remains constant unless the spindle is damaged during use.

independent suspension - suspension in which each wheel can travel up-and-down without directly affecting the position of the opposite wheel.

integral power steering - a unit designed with the vehicle. It typically incorporates a hydraulic pump and a steering gear where the pump's hydraulic fluid directly puts pressure on and helps actuate the mechanical parts in doing the work of steering the vehicle.

--k--

key - a pin, bolt, wedge, cotter or similar device put into a hole, channel or space to lock or hold parts together; a small block inserted between the shaft and hub to prevent circumferential movement.

keyway - slot cut into a shaft to accept a key.

kingpin inclination - the kingpins (or knuckle support pivots) are inclined toward each other at the top. This angle is known as kingpin inclination and is usually spoken of, and measured, in degrees. The effect of kingpin inclination is to cause the wheels to steer in a straight line, regardless of outside forces such as crowned roads, cross winds, etc., which may tend to make the vehicle steer at a tangent. It does this, in effect, by removing the lever arm that would exist between the centerline of the wheel and the centerline of the steering knuckle if the knuckle were vertical.

kneeback - a kneeback means that one complete side of the front suspension is bent back. This is often caused by crimping the front wheels against the curb when parking the vehicle, then starting up without straightening the wheels out.

knuckle - suspension component that connects the upper and lower control arms or the strut and lower control arm. Also called a steering knuckle.

--l--

lateral runout - side-to-side movement or wobble in a wheel or tire.

live axle - (also called tag axle) allows a truck to handle increased loads by using an additional non-powered axle either in front or behind the drive axle(s). Lift axles can be utilized on trucks, trailers, or both depending on the need. This additional axle is normally raised off the ground when not in use.

Glossary of Terms

live axle - axle on which the wheels are firmly affixed, with the axle driving the wheels.

load range - letter code system that indicates the weight carrying capacity of tires.

lubrication - process of introducing a friction reducing substance between moving parts to reduce wear.

lug-type tires - lug tires have discrete block-like sections of tread designed to help the truck gain traction in mud and snow. They are most often used in the drive axle positions.

--m--

memory steer - steering condition where the steering wheel and wheels want to return to a position other than center. This can be caused by tightening rubber bonded socket tie-rod ends when the steering wheel is not centered, binding in the upper strut mounts, or binding in a steering component or ball joint.

--n--

National Institute for Automotive Service Excellence (ASE, formerly NIASE) - nonprofit certification agency for automotive, truck, school bus, auto body, engine machine shop and parts personnel.

normal wear - average expected wear when operating under normal conditions.

--o--

outer bearing race - outer part of a ball or roller bearing that provides a surface for the balls or rollers to rotate. Can be integral with the bearing or a separate part.

--p--

parallelogram steering linkage - type of conventional steering linkage consisting of a pitman arm, centerlink, idler arm and tie-rod assemblies to connect to the steering knuckles. The pitman arm, centerlink and idler arm form three sides of a parallelogram.

pintle hook - coupling device used in double trailer, triple trailer and truck-trailer combinations. It has a curved, fixed towing horn with an upper latch that opens to accept the drawbar eye of a trailer dolly.

pitman arm - steering system component mounted on the steering box shaft and transfers the gearbox motion to the steering linkage.

power cylinder - part of a semi-integral power steering unit that applies mechanical pressure to the steering gear using either hydraulic or pneumatic pressure.

press fit - when a part is slightly larger than a hole it must be forced together with a press

pressure relief valve - a valve located in the power steering pump or steering gear and designed to limit pressure to a preset figure. When pressure passes the required setting, fluid is bypassed from the pump output back to a return line or circuit. Such valves are used to protect system seals from excessive pressure and consequent wear.

pressure test - a test of a power steering pump's ability to provide adequate fluid pressure. Lack of pressure will frequently cause power steering performance complaints. Lack of pressure may occur due to wear of internal pump parts or failure of the pressure relief valve.

pull-around torque - this refers to the torque required to rotate a nut, as in torquing the nuts fastening a U-bolt that retains a stack of spring leaves.

pull-up torque - the torque actually applied to retain an assembly such as a spring stack. Even if the pull-around torque applied to a spring stack or other component is correct, the pull-up torque may not be.

--r--

radial-ply tires - radial tires have belts or cords that run from bead to bead directly along the radius of the tire. They were developed as tire cord materials became stronger to provide tires with the most flexible possible casing. This maximizes the tread's contact with the road (minimizing tread squirm as the tire rotates). By enabling the casing to flex more easily, fuel economy is maximized and heat minimized.

radial runout - out-of-roundness of a wheel or tire.

Glossary of Terms

radius arm - suspension component that is connected to a twin I-beam or solid axle at one end and to the vehicle frame through bushings at the other. The radius arm braces the I-beam or axle and keeps it at a right angle to the vehicle frame.

rebound - expansion of a suspension spring after it has been compressed.

recirculating ball steering - steering gear in which steering movement is transmitted by a worm gear and ball nut. A set of ball bearings rolls in the grooves between the worm gear and ball nut in a continuous loop.

rib-type tires - rib tires have a tread pattern designed to maximize fuel economy. The pattern runs continuously around the tire's circumference in a relatively simple ring configuration. Rib tires may be used in any position but are usually not preferred in drive positions except in climates without snow and ice.

roll stiffness - resistance to allowing the truck to roll over or to lean into turns. Good air suspension systems often exhibit high roll stiffness in spite of offering a soft ride.

roller bearing - anti-friction device made up of hardened inner and outer races between which steel rollers move.

rotor pump - type of oil pump that utilizes a 4-lobe inner rotor and a 5-lobe outer rotor. Output per revolution depends upon rotor diameter and thickness.

runout - wobble or deflection beyond a rotating part's normal plane of movement.

--s--

safety valve - air power steering units have an air safety valve. This valve closes automatically whenever brake system reservoir pressure drops below 65 psi. A manual valve is also included and can be used to isolate the steering system from the brake system in case of steering system leaks.

scalloping - tire wear pattern (caused by wheel imbalance) in which pieces appear to be cut out of the tire by a spoon.

scrub radius - distance between the point at which the tire's vertical centerpoint intersects the road, and the steering axis inclination (SAI) intersects the road.

semi-integral power steering - a unit installed on an existing vehicle built with manual steering. Typically, steering requirements are measured through a replacement steering drag link or tie-rod as it is compressed or stretched as the wheel is turned. The steering system is assisted through a hydraulic or air cylinder.

short and long arm suspension - suspension system with the upper arm shorter than the lower arm, allowing the wheel to deflect in a vertical direction with minimal change in camber.

sliding fifth wheel - fore-and-aft adjustable fifth wheel that is designed to enable even distribution of the trailer weight.

solid rim (or continuous rim) - refers to a type of wheel rim used only with tubeless-type tires. The rim does not split because of the need to make it absolutely airtight. The tire's outer bead seals against the rim on either side and the tire's casing is designed to be airtight, thus eliminating the need for a separate, air pressure containing tube. The outer bead of the tire is designed to be strong enough to retain its shape and prevent the air pressure from blowing the tire off the rim. Because of the high risk inherent in bead damage with such a tire/rim system, special tools and operating techniques are essential when working with this type rim.

spindle - shaft used to attach the wheel assembly on non-drive axles.

split-rim - a type of wheel/rim system used with tube-type tires. The rim actually has a ring, which separates from the rim itself once the tire is deflated. Split rims make mounting and demounting easier, but require extremely careful inspection and assembly for safe operation. When properly assembled, the pressure within the tube and tire keeps the split rim securely assembled.

spring rate - spring rate is the rate at which a spring supporting force increases as it is compressed. Springs with high spring rates support heavy loads well but yield a harsh ride. Springs with low spring rates give a smooth ride but do not work well on axles where the total weight carried varies a great deal. Front-axle springs often have relatively low spring rates.

stabilizer bar - torsion-bar spring connecting the suspension on either side of the vehicle. When a vehicle rolls to the side in a turn, the suspension at the outside wheel compresses and the suspension at the inside wheel extends. The stabilizer bar that connects them twists to

Glossary of Terms

apply a counteracting force to hold the vehicle closer to level. Also called an anti-roll bar or sway bar.

stack settling - stack settling refers to the behavior of a stack of leaf springs after assembly and torquing of the U-bolt. The stack tends to compress, actually occupying less space. This causes loosening of the retaining parts, relative movement between the leaves and consequent wear. It can be prevented by proper retorquing of U-bolt retaining nuts.

static balance - balance at rest; still balance; the equal distribution of weight of the wheel and tire around the axis of rotation such that the wheel assembly has no tendency to rotate by itself regardless of its position.

steering arm - steering system component that links the steering knuckle to the tie-rod assembly.

steering axis inclination - angle between true vertical and an imaginary line running through the rotational center of the ball joint(s).

steering column - housing, steering shaft, bearings and related components between the steering wheel and the steering gear.

steering gear - assembly located at the end of the steering column, which contains the gears and other components that multiply the driver turning force.

steering linkage - all of the components that connect the steering gear to the front wheels.

strut rod - on vehicles where the lower control arm is attached to the frame at one pivot point, a strut rod is used to brace the control arm against the vehicle frame.

--t--

tandem axles - two single-axle assemblies, one behind the other.

Technology and Maintenance Council (TMC) - formerly named The Maintenance Council. Branch of the American Trucking Associations dedicated to providing technology solutions to the trucking industry through education, networking, and standards development.

tie-rod - steering linkage member that connects the steering knuckle arm with the centerlink or the steering rack.

tie-rod end - ball and socket joint that connects the tie-rod to the steering knuckle arm and to the centerlink or steering rack.

tire rotation - practice of moving a set of tires to different positions on the vehicle to equalize wear and extend the life of the tires.

tire scrub - condition of suspension or wheel maintenance that causes tires to rub along a road surface rather than rolling. Tandem rear-axle tires naturally tend to scrub slightly in a turn. When a drive or trailer axle is not parallel to the front axle, tire scrubbing will occur.

toe-in - toe-in is the amount that the front wheels are closer together at the front than they are at the back. This dimension is usually spoken of, and measured in inches or fractions of an inch. Toe-in performs the function of preloading steering linkage joints and counteracts the wheel's positive camber tendency to pull outwards at the front.

torque steer - tendency of a vehicle to turn somewhat from the desired direction when accelerating, especially in a curve, or when decelerating in a curve.

torque valve - a torque valve is an integral part of a modified drag link (or in some cases a modified tie-rod) that replaces the original drag link when a semi-integral, air-assisted power steering unit is installed. The torque valve senses pressure on the wheel (movement) by changing its length very slightly. This, in turn, meters air to a power cylinder.

torsion bar - bar made of spring steel that uses a twisting motion to support the weight of the vehicle and absorb road shock.

--u--

U-bolt - U-shaped fastener that is used to clamp spring assembly and rear axle together.

underslung suspension - suspension system where the spring assembly is mounted under the axle.

unsprung weight - components of a vehicle that rest directly on the road surface without being supported by the suspension springs.

Glossary of Terms

--w--

wheel alignment - adjustment of suspension and steering components to optimize steering control and minimize tire wear.

wheel balance - condition in which a wheel/tire assembly has equal weight around its center, preventing vibration at high speeds. Wheel balance can be static, such as on a bubble balancer, or dynamic, such as with a spin balancer.

wheel offset - dimensional difference between a wheel's centerline and the plane of the axle flange mounting surface.

wheel slip - measurement (in percentage) of the friction between the tire and road surface; at zero slip the tire rotates freely, while at 100% slip the tire is locked up and is pushed along the road surface by the moving vehicle. Also called tire slip.

wheel weights - small weights, usually made of lead, attached either mechanically or by adhesive to a wheel/tire assembly to correct its balance.

--y--

yield point - the point where a bolt starts to lose its strength as it is stretched. Bolts fastening spring leaves together are typically torqued past their elastic limit and just to the yield point. This stretches the bolt very slightly but actually enables the bolt to handle more torque than it could if it had not been stretched. However, if torqued past the yield point, the bolt would actually lose its ability to retain torque and hold the spring leaves together.